TREASURE HUNTS

TREASURE HUNTS

What My Son Taught Me from the Other Side and How I Learned to Hear Him

Lisa Frankel

10th House Publishers

Treasure Hunts. What My Son Taught Me From the Other Side and How I Learned to Hear Him.

Cover design: Evan Fila
Author photos: faiellastudios.com
Edited by: Caitlin Anders

Published by 10th House Publishers
1733 Route 9
Clifton Park, NY 12065
www.10thhp.com

ISBN (Paperback): 9798999505217

Author's Note

(Disclaimer)

The stories in this book are retellings of events as I experienced and remember them. They reflect my own perspective, memory, and interpretation, and are not meant as a precise factual record or professional advice.

To respect the privacy of others, some names have been shortened to initials, and in a few places, dates or identifying details have been adjusted. If you happen to recognize yourself in these pages where I have not named you directly, I hope you receive it as part of the story I've lived and remembered. Any errors are entirely my own.

I dedicate this book
To my husband Jeff, and my sons Jayson, Justin, and Matty. You are my heart.

And to anyone navigating grief, hope, or simply seeking deeper connection—these pages offer a reminder that the ones we love are closer than we realize.

Sometimes the veil between worlds grows thin.
Sometimes the ones we love send little
treasures to remind us:
"I'm still here."

Scan, scroll, and there I am with a message
just for you!

TABLE OF CONTENTS

Introduction

Part One
My World Changed

Part Two
Starting to Hear

Prologue

Spirit likes to wake me with messages. In the beginning, they were just for me, whispered loud and clear in my left ear. Over time, the messages began arriving for the people I'd soon be reading for. Eventually, with a little negotiation, Spirit agreed to shift most of this to the daytime (thankfully, because I do love my sleep!). A few of those messages circled around the idea of writing a book.

At first, the thought of writing felt overwhelming. But Matty, my son on the other side, had different plans. He came through to my sister-in-law, Gayle, on many occasions, nudging me through her with questions like: "When are you writing the book?" and "How's the book coming?" Those questions carried a strange mixture of feelings I hadn't known before: incredulousness, procrastination, self-doubt, and complete awe.

When I finally began, meditation helped me find the words. Very quickly, I realized I wasn't writing this book alone—Matty was guiding me.

How can I be so sure? The night before I handed my complete manuscript to a friend for a final read-through, I was woken in the middle of the night by one of those crystal-clear messages:

Bears and Tattoos and The Unveiling

The words repeated until I got up and wrote them down. Curious, I went to the printed manuscript. To my shock, I discovered I had forgotten to include *two whole stories*. They were sitting in my edited file, but I had neglected to move them into the final version. That unmistakable feeling washed over me, the one that tells me Matty is near. My jaw dropped.

That was my reminder. Matty isn't just my co-creator or co-author. He might very well be *the* author, writing this book through me, for you.

How amazing is that?

TREAUSRE HUNTS

Some treasures don't glint in the sun or sparkle on a shelf. Some treasures live in the softest places—inside a sudden breeze, a stray song lyric, a dragonfly that lands too close to be a coincidence.

After losing my son, Matty, I began living what I can only call a series of treasure hunts. At first, I didn't know what I was looking for. I only knew I was desperate for a sign that he was still somewhere, somehow with me.

What I found—and continue to find—are moments of breathtaking, playful, tender connection. Moments that invite me to live with my heart wide open to magic, even inside grief.

This book is a small collection of those treasures. True stories. Ordinary days made extraordinary by love that refuses to leave. I offer them to you as gentle proof that bonds of the heart don't break; they simply change shape. May you find your own treasures, too.

Part One

When my world changed, everything else did too. Grief cracked me open, but in the quiet after the storm, something unexpected began to unfold. Signs. Dreams. A feeling that I wasn't alone. I didn't know the rules, or even what I believed anymore—but I began to pay attention. And in doing so, I started to learn the language of love that continues beyond this life.

What Are Treasure Hunts?

A Treasure Hunt is a series of connected signs from my loved ones on the Other Side, all forming under a common theme or message. They don't usually show up all at once—they unfold over time. Sometimes, within a single day, other times stretching across several. But when a Treasure Hunt begins, I can feel it. The signs stand out— unmistakable and deliberate—as if lit up against the haze of everyday life.

My body reacts before my brain does. A swirl in my belly. A tingling at the back of my head. A pause. That internal, *huh* . . . when something catches me just enough to stop and take notice. It's grounding and ungrounding at the same time.

The very first Treasure Hunt came on 3-22-2023—a date that may seem ordinary at first glance. But the number 222 had already been showing up in my life long before my son Matty crossed over. A quiet nudge from the universe I didn't yet understand.

Matty crossed on 8-18-2022 at the age of 21. In the months that followed, the signs kept coming—222 among them. I began recording them in a journal. Each connection. Each blink of recognition. Each moment made me stop and wonder. Looking back now, I see

what I couldn't see then: these weren't just coincidences. They were pieces of a map.

These experiences weren't just happening *to* me. They were being laid out *for* me. Not only so I could find them, but so I could share them.

Every Treasure Hunt is a marvel. A small miracle that leaves me awestruck. I write them down to remember, to relive, and—more importantly—to pass along. Because these gifts aren't just for me. They're meant to be shared.

I never imagined that grief could lead to this kind of connection. But Spirit doesn't just want to comfort us. It wants to surprise us. To make us laugh. To bring lightness. To remind us—again and again—that love doesn't end.

When the clues finally come together, it's like a bolt of lightning in a dark sky. And there I stand, jaw dropped, the last puzzle piece clicking into place.

Smiling.

Stunned.

And—rare for me—completely speechless.

Opening the Veil: A Mother's Journey Begins

Walking has always been my refuge. Even as a teenager, I'd go out alone, lost in my thoughts, walking until something inside me felt complete. Later in life, I cherished walking with a close friend, sharing everything about our kids, jobs, and families, solving the world's problems together from A to Z.

But on August 18, 2022, my world shattered. It wasn't just grief—it was like being trapped inside a shaken snow globe, my entire existence thrown into disarray. I needed to walk more than ever, but the thought of company was unbearable. I needed solitude. I needed my dog.

Grizzly, ever eager for a walk, didn't mind when I grabbed his leash at 4:30 AM those first mornings. Thank goodness the streets were deserted. In those early days, when I could barely stop crying, the solitude was a gift.

We were living in a temporary apartment at the time, and as we rode the elevator down, Grizzly already knew the route. He always started out briskly. I don't remember if it was that first morning or the second, but I stopped him, standing still under the vast sky.

I spoke out loud, my voice breaking in the quiet: "To all or any who are listening over there . . . I know there are people who can communicate with the other side. And

3

now I need to be one of them. I will be a receiver. I will do whatever it takes, because my son lives there now and I need to talk to him, just like I did when he was here."

I stood there, the weight of my words settling around me. And I *believed*—deep in my bones—that they heard me. My loved ones. The universe. The powers that be.

And then I *saw* it.

To the left of my head, just beyond my shoulder, a sheer, white, curtain-like veil. And it flew open.

I gasped. I saw it as clearly as anything in front of me.

Out loud, I whispered: "The veil has opened."

I took a deep breath, steadied myself, and walked on.

The next morning, at 4:30 AM, we set out again. The stillness outside was almost soothing to the chaotic storm inside me. Grizzly, for some reason, insisted we take our usual loop *backward*. He pulled against me when I tried to turn him around.

"Alright," I sighed. "We'll do it your way."

We started with the wooded path instead of ending there, looped through the parking lot, and finally onto the sidewalk that led home.

That's when I saw him.

A man, walking toward us from a distance. My first thought was, *Who else is out here at this hour?*

As he got closer, something was . . . off.

He wasn't dressed for this time. He wore green polyester pants, a red-and-white striped polo, and a straw hat. Dark hair. A distinct presence.

And as we passed each other, he locked eyes with me. He nodded slowly, deliberately.

I kept walking. And then—

"Jay?"

I spun around. He was gone.

Jay—my father-in-law—who had passed over thirty years ago at the age of 51.

Oh my God.

A buzz of energy shot through me. I jogged home, burst through the door, and said to my husband, breathless, "I just saw your dad."

He just smiled.

I wrote in my journal that night:

"Thank you, Jay, for letting me know you're around. I'm happy you get to be with Matty. You'll love him. Jealous, though."

When I told my mediumship teacher about it later, he called it an apparition.

Oh. Okay, then.

The day of Matty's funeral, we hired a van to take us to the temple and cemetery. None of us could have handled driving.

I couldn't even look out the window. I closed my eyes, trying to block out the unbearable reality of where we were going.

And then—

I *felt* them.

On my right, my mother, her bright, swirling light beside me. One arm across my stomach, the other stretched behind my back, holding me up.

On my left, my grandfather, facing me, his hand resting gently on my leg.

I didn't question it. I just whispered in my mind: *Thank God you're here.*

And I let them hold me.

Who knew that in a moment of unimaginable pain, my mother and grandfather—both gone for over 25 years—could show up in a van bound for my youngest son's funeral . . . and hold me together?

A week later, we had to visit our new home to take measurements.

The last time we'd been there, Matty was with us.

That visit had been perfect—laughter, excitement, all of us dreaming about the future. And now? Now, we were four people, hollow and shattered.

We finished what we needed to do. Everyone else got into their cars. But I just . . . stood in the driveway.

I screamed in my head: *How can I live here? I don't know how to do this.*

And then—

A wave of peace, slow and deliberate, rolled down from the top of my head to the tips of my toes. It felt like a blanket unfurling, covering me, calming my breath.

And a voice, clear as day, whispered:

"It's okay to live here."

I didn't question it.

I wiped my tears, took a deep breath, and got in the car.

In the weeks that followed, I started going back to an exercise class. I needed movement. Two friends met me there, making it slightly easier.

Still, the questions haunted me. *How can you do anything that brings even a sliver of joy when your son just died?*

And then, in the middle of class, another whisper came:

"I'm glad you're here."

I smiled.

Okay.

Not long after that, I was walking Grizzly again in the dark, where I could cry freely, unseen.

And another whisper came:

"Go to yoga. Breathe deeply."

Okay.

I went that Saturday.

People often ask me how mediumship came into my life. Have you always had this?

Now I know the answer.

Yes. In ways I never recognized before.

Through grief, I've learned about energy, consciousness, and my own way of moving through this world. Those first connections—the veil opening, Jay, my mother and grandfather holding me, G. Gram, the whispers—were all signposts, guiding me forward.

And I wanted more.

So, I set out on a journey of learning.

One that still continues today.

The First Week

I don't remember much from those first days after that horrible, horrible night. Grief swallowed me whole— mind, body, soul. I asked a friend to bring me a journal, and when I look back now, the first entry reads:

"Whenever grief arises, drop the storyline and rest with this powerful emotion. Let grief wash over me and dissipate. It is not solid . . . It is fluid."

I don't remember writing that. I wonder now if it helped.

It was the beginning of a new way of being. The day after the funeral. I wrote: *BE and let BE,* as if I might find my footing there, somehow.

I noted that I received a text early that morning. My first thought was—*It's Matty.* But no. He was no longer here. That realization hit like a new wound. *Slow down and breathe,* I wrote.

Later: *There's a hole in me.* Maybe I don't want it to be filled. Maybe it can't be. Matty lived in that space, and now it feels uninhabitable. How do I carry this? How do I live beside it?

And then a quieter truth followed: Not to avoid it. Not to pretend it isn't there. But to live with it.

The next day, only three words: *Dread. Pain. Regret.* Conversations I wished I'd had. Things I wished I'd done differently. All I could do was breathe. *How can I? Time,* I answered.

A few days later, something unexpected surfaced: I can feel two things at once. Sadness and curiosity. Sadness and calm. Sadness and, somehow, the flicker of happiness.

Then came the guilt. *How can I feel anything good when my son just died?*

Dread returned, and with it, the questions that wouldn't let go: Is he safe? Is he feeling love? Is he scared? Has he found Bear?

Who met you when you transitioned, Matty? Were you afraid? Confused? My heart aches at the thought that you might have been scared. Are you peaceful now? I miss you so, so much.

How can this be?

There are moments I want to scream—an unfiltered, guttural cry from deep within. How can this be?

My Matty is on the other side.

And still, even in this unraveling, something else stirs.

Everything feels different now. My phone is quiet. No more sweet texts. No more calls. That steady rhythm of love and reassurance—just gone.

I'm scared to scroll back through our messages. Afraid to remember what I can't receive again.

But I think you're with Grandpa Alan. You'll love him. He's loved you your whole life. And Grandma Susan, too. And your G. Gram. You're safe. You'll shine. You'll dazzle, like you always did. You'll figure it all out.

You were made of light, Matty. I know that hasn't changed.

Maybe you're already reaching out.

I've always known bees meant Grandma Susan. Repeating numbers—2:22, 4:44—have been Grandpa's way of saying hello. Those signs brought me comfort. But now, when I see them, I pause.

Are they holding you close?

And if they are . . . why does it ache?

There it is: comfort and jealousy, wrapped tight in my chest. I want them to hold you. I want you to be safe. But I want you here.

Still, deep down, I know: You will shine on the other side.

And you and I?

We'll figure out our connection. I promise, Matty. We'll do our work—together.

A Chain of Signs

One weekend morning, not long after the world turned upside down, I was on the phone with my sister-in-law, Gayle. She has always had a strong intuitive side. She's been receiving signs for years, and they increased a lot after Matty crossed over. We often talk about these moments, sharing the connections as they unfold. That morning, Gayle was telling me about a sign she had just received from her father, who had passed away 19 years ago.

Gayle has a love for word puzzles, especially *The Jumble*, a daily newspaper puzzle where you unscramble letters to form words and solve a final puzzle phrase. She never misses a day. That morning, when she sat down with her coffee and opened the puzzle, she couldn't believe her eyes—every word was connected to her dad: Mort (his name), Dad, and even Dead (she chuckled at that one). It felt as if he was saying hello through the puzzle she loved so much.

As Gayle shared this with me, I stood at my bedroom window, looking outside. Mid-sentence, a cardinal and a bluejay flew onto my windowsill, both of them staring directly at me. I froze. At that moment, the cardinal was an unmistakable sign from Matty, and the bluejay—a connection to my father-in-law, Jay.

"I see my cardinal—Matty! And the bluejay—Jay!" I blurted out.

The cardinal hopped onto the roof, and as I scrambled for my phone to take a picture, it buzzed with a text. It was from one of Matty's good friends, sharing the signs he'd been receiving. His message read:

"Matty has been showing up recently. Last week, I won NE10 player of the week, and my stat line was 2 goals and 6 wins (26). After our first four games, I've racked up 26 points. I know that's him walking with me this season, and spiritually, he's as present as ever!!"

Matty wore number 26 in lacrosse.

I stood there, stunned.

After hanging up with Gayle, I walked into my son Justin's room to say goodbye before leaving for the day. His clock read 11:11. Since Matty crossed over, I've always seen 11:11 as a reminder to trust my intuition.

I went downstairs, took my time putting on my shoes, and as I did, a sliver of doubt crept in. Really, Lisa? Maybe it's just a coincidence—the birds, the text, the call, all happening like this.

Finally, I stepped into my car and started the engine. The dashboard clock lit up: 11:11.

At that exact moment, Adam Levine's song "Memories" came on the radio.

"*Here's to the ones that we love, here's to the ones that we've lost on the way . . .*"

A wave of knowing washed over me. I smiled and said aloud, "OK, Matty. I see them all, and I love you for sending them."

Treasure Hunts

As I drove down the highway, I spotted two different license plates with 111, then a bumper sticker with 26, and finally, my eyes were drawn to a mile marker—111.

Alright, Matty . . . no more doubting.

On this particular day, everything seemed to fall into place all at once, like a series of random moments aligning to create a powerful, unmistakable message from Matty. It was as if the universe had orchestrated a chain of signs, each one leading to the next, all coming together in one big "Hello, I'm here." In the span of just a few minutes, the signs flowed in a way I couldn't ignore—a cardinal perched on my windowsill, a message from one of Matty's friends, and the unmistakable synchronicity of numbers—all connecting me back to him. Each sign was a thread in a larger tapestry, each one reinforcing the feeling that Matty was right there, still walking beside me.

The Five of Wands

The deposition is coming up. I will be sitting across from a lawyer representing a strained and troubled system—one that couldn't hold what mattered most. My world had already split wide open, and now I have to recount the five days leading up to my son's last breath, taken in my arms. This haunts me.

I've worked hard to stay attuned to the sensations in my body; to be open so I can connect with my son and my loved ones on the other side. But the density of this moment, the darkness, and the weight of anticipation press on me. I feel it more intensely because of the work I've done to stay open. The closer the deposition gets, the more I feel like I'm sinking.

A month or so ago, I decided to offer tarot readings. I have a wonderful teacher, and I'm drawn to the magic of the cards. To practice, I offered free readings for a month. I probably did about ten. And in nearly every reading, the Five of Wands appeared. At first, I saw it as a message for the person I was reading for, but the frequency of it nagged at me. Maybe it was speaking to me, too. Still, I wasn't convinced.

Then, one day, I sat in my office, heavy-hearted. I had been working hard to counterbalance the suffocating dread of sitting in that chair, being questioned. I meditated. I worked on letting go. I tried to shut down the relentless thoughts that tempted me into rabbit holes—those torturous "what-ifs" that suggested a different outcome was possible. I talked with my therapist. I exercised. And yet . . . the weight remained.

That day, I suddenly thought, *Pull a card for yourself.*

I shuffled my deck and asked, "What do I need to know today?"

A card flew out and landed on the floor.

The Five of Wands.

No denying it now. It was for me too.

I closed my eyes and moved into meditation, pen in hand, ready to receive guidance. I asked, "What does this card mean for me?"

The words came:

You have a broken heart. That can get in the way. Things you have not fully addressed may surface as fear or trauma. The lawyer will embody values you do not align with. This may confuse you—if you let it. Be still. Be wise. Be you. All of you. Just be. Don't try to align. Allow the discomfort. It is important to get this right.

I hesitated at that last word—*right.* I rarely receive that word in guidance. Later, in reflection, I realized they didn't mean "right" as in winning or proving something. They meant *allowing.* Allowing the truth. Allowing what is.

Then Auntie Helen appeared. My great-aunt, my tarot guide. She read cards when she was here, and now she guides me from the other side. Her voice, familiar and strong:

Dolly, the Five of Wands means freedom. Freedom from strife. Look to the stars—so many, so many ways to go, to choose. Allow, without judgment. Without prescribing how it should unfold. The card shows five men lifting their wands together. It's not just you. It's not up to you. It's the compilation of all the forces that create the outcome. You are a cog, a wheel in the machine. Welcome to the machine.

I exhaled. A Pink Floyd reference. A sign. My mother and I have shared this sign since she passed 26 years ago.

It unsettled me.

I asked, "What do I do with the resurfacing of all that occurred?"

Auntie Helen's answer was simple. *Nothing. All you can do is answer the questions.*

I asked, "Is there anything else I should know?"

The answer: *It would have been anyway. And so it will be.*

I reached for my tarot book, needing to see what it said. The Five of Wands: *For those who do not wish to engage in fighting, a moment of truth may be upon you. Will you stand up for what is right? Can you express your thoughts without harming those who oppose you? Can you surrender to the situation yet remain strong?*

Then a quote from Eckhart Tolle:

"Accept your here and now totally by dropping all inner resistance. The false, unhappy self that loves feeling miserable, resentful, or sorry for itself can no longer survive. This is called surrender. Surrender is not weakness. There is great strength in it."

Helen's words. The book's wisdom. It all wove together. I have never been one for conflict. Even in my career, I chose collaboration over confrontation. And now, here I was, in a battle I never wanted but had no choice but to fight.

The deposition day came. I tucked the Five of Wands into my purse. A talisman. A reminder.

I carried Auntie Helen's words, my guides' wisdom, and the message of the card.

It was not just me.

I was a cog in the machine. A part of a whole.

And I told the story. Every bit of it. I let the emotions rise and fall as they needed to.

Because it is my story.

My truth.

Lisa Frankel

Signs in Song Lyrics

In the beginning, I wasn't sure what to think. Like many people, I had a surface-level understanding of signs—something you might hear about or wish for but not necessarily trust. When Matty crossed over, I desperately wanted signs and connection, but I didn't know if it was even possible. I questioned everything. Was that a sign? Am I making this up? If I ask too much, will I block them? Will my grief keep him from growing? My journal is filled with these questions, a mix of longing and uncertainty.

My beginning journaling came mostly in the form of questions: *Did you try to show me a sign? Are you there in love and light? Will I forget things—stages of your life that I can no longer reminisce with you about? I saw a dragonfly. Was this a sign? If you stay close to me and show me signs, am I inhibiting your journey on the other side? If I tell you I'm OK, will that help your growth over there? What if my grief and sadness overtake me?*

My mediumship mentor gave me advice that settled into my heart: Matty had to learn to live *there*, and I had to learn to live *here*. And in that space between, we had to develop our own way of communicating. I wanted so badly to hold on, to feel him close in the ways I had before, but our connection had to evolve. He wasn't gone, but he wasn't here in the way I was used to.

I devoured books on signs, on the afterlife, on mediumship. I read about near-death experiences and mothers who had lost children, searching for any proof that our connection could continue. I wanted to believe it, but I wasn't there yet.

Then, the lyrics started.

At first, I didn't know what to make of them. I would wake up in the middle of the night with just a single line looping in my head. Not a full song, not something I could immediately place—just a lyric. I struggled to hear the rest, trying to identify the artist, the meaning, the reason it was there. One book suggested keeping a pen and paper by my bed, so I started writing them down in the dark. The first one repeated for nights on end: "*Conceived in love, sun is gonna shine above.*" Loggins and Messina. Not in my playlists. Not a song I had any memory of choosing.

Then came another. And another. Soon, a pattern emerged.

One morning, I ran into my friend, the same friend who had given me messages from my mother and grandmother before Matty passed. She had something to tell me. "I have a song lyric looping in my head, and I'm pretty sure it's for you," she said.

"What is it?" I asked, my heart racing.

"*Ohh, Susie Q, honey, I love you.*"

My mother's name is Susan.

I couldn't deny it anymore. These lyrics weren't random. They were messages. Someone, somewhere, was reaching for me.

A new lyric would come almost every night. "*Free your mind, and the rest will follow.*" Not in my playlist. A reminder to quiet my thoughts, to let go, to be open. Then: "*I Will Survive.*" A declaration of resilience. Then: "*We're out of the woods, out of the woods . . .*" from *The Wizard of Oz*, flashing in my mind with the vibrant green of the Emerald City. Was *I* out of the woods? Was Matty? I didn't know, but I thanked Spirit for the message anyway.

My mediumship teacher told me to look for patterns. That our skeptical minds would try to explain these things away, but when the same kind of sign shows up again and again, it becomes undeniable. And it was happening to me. These lyrics weren't songs I had been listening to; they weren't pulled from my personal playlists, and yet they were arriving, one after another, each carrying meaning, each offering love and reassurance.

Still, I hesitated. Could I ask for one? Would that be too much? One night, I decided to try. As I drifted off to sleep, I whispered in my mind, "Mom, please, I need a connection. Will you send me a lyric?"

I woke up to: "*Time is on my side, yes it is.*" The Rolling Stones. Thank you, Mom.

Eventually, I began to trust it. The lyrics became something I looked forward to, little glimpses of connection, moments where I could breathe. And then, as I was falling asleep, an image came into my mind so vibrant I had to get up and draw it.

It looked like mylar balloons, big and silver, gently floating. And then, the lyric came that took my breath away: *"Yesterday, a child came out to wander. Caught a dragonfly inside a jar."*

"The Circle Game." Joni Mitchell.

A dragonfly. *Our* sign.

Matty.

I had not thought of that song since seventh grade. And yet, there it was, unmistakable.

He had found a way to reach me. I thanked him, sobbing, overwhelmed by the sheer brilliance of it all. They *are* clever, our loved ones. They *are* with us.

I have pages and pages of lyrics now, and I love every single one of them. They don't erase the pain, but they carve out space to breathe. They help me have a moment of calm amidst all the heaviness. And they give me hope in a multitude of ways that are hard to articulate.

This I do know—we are not alone. Connection is real. Love never ends.

Bears and Tattoos

When I turned 50, I made a bit of a bucket list. One of the first entries? Get a dog. My three boys were pre-teen and teenagers at the time, and you can imagine the chaos in our house. I thought a dog might bring us all together in a new way - maybe even mellow things out.

I chose a tiny, all-black male Havanese. No one wanted him quite like I did. I named him Bear. He was the cutest three-pound fluffball, and we all pitched in to help him settle into our family. It didn't take long for Bear to pick his favorite sleeping spot. Every night, without fail, he'd curl up on Matty's legs like it was the only place in the world he wanted to be. Just like that, bears and bear paws became a symbol of love and connection in our family.

We adored Bear for six years until the unimaginable happened. One day, while Matty was walking him, a distracted driver ended Bear's time with us far too soon. Matty lay down on the road beside him, looking into his sweet eyes as he crossed the Rainbow Bridge. It was a devastating loss. Matty later told me he could still feel Bear with him, even see him sometimes. And every time he did, it made him smile. Somehow, that comforted us all.

A bear paw became a symbol for Matty, and he proudly displayed one on his lacrosse helmet for all the years he played goalie. When we got a new puppy shortly after

Bear's crossing, we all agreed Matty should name him. And he did—Grizzly Bearcub.

Years later, we moved into a temporary apartment, all five of us (plus Grizzly) crammed into a space that was never meant to hold that much life. During this time, I had to find a new dog boarding place. It was . . . not a great choice. Grizzly managed to escape, and while I drove five hours home, determined to find him, I called on Bear for help. I could feel his sweet presence hovering over my shoulder as I drove, whispering reassurance. As we neared the boarding site, I spoke out loud: "Bear, go find Grizzly!"

When we pulled up, rain poured down, and there was Grizzly, sitting on the porch, drenched but waiting. He jumped into my arms the second I reached him. Home we went.

Another year passed, and another loss came; one I could never have prepared for. Losing Matty shook my world to its core. Grief settled in deep, and I wondered if I would ever feel whole again.

We decided to get a family tattoo. The day before the funeral, when I told my sister-in-law about it, she said, "Matty says, 'What about me?'" So, I sketched a design that felt right to all of us and tucked a copy into Matty's hoodie in his final resting place.

The day we went to get our tattoos, the air was crisp and bright, the kind of September day that almost fools you into believing everything is okay. As I walked alone to the tattoo shop, I silently asked, "Matty, will you come with us?"

As I walked, a street singer caught my attention. The world around me seemed to slow, and she locked eyes with me. She paused, then began to sing "Amazing Grace." Her voice was hauntingly beautiful, and for a moment, the rest of the world blurred, and it felt like she was singing just for me. Tears welled in my eyes. *Okay, Matty. Thank you for the song.*

Inside the tattoo shop, my family was already gathered. As we settled in, I chatted with Rick, the artist. A song played in the background, something that sounded an awful lot like The Grateful Dead.

"Is this The Dead?" I asked.

Rick grinned. "Yeah, I used to travel with them for a while."

Of course he did.

Then, a group of teenagers burst into the shop, loud and giggling, clearly not there for tattoos. Rick teased one of the girls about needing a parent's permission. As she passed by us, she turned, looked right at me, and said, "Hi, my name is Maddie." And just like that, I knew. My son was with us.

We wear our tattoos proudly, a symbol of love, connection, and the undeniable ways Matty had begun to find us, over and over again.

Lisa Frankel

THEIRS:

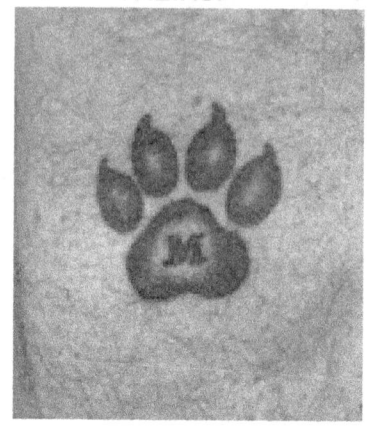

MINE:

MATTY'S:

Grief and the Art of Asking

I've learned a lot about grief. It is not just an emotion or a state of being—it feels like an entity, something alive and shifting, with its own rhythm and presence. Sometimes it moves like a quiet current, barely noticeable, and other times it crashes in, demanding to be felt. I've come to understand that grief is not linear, nor is it something to be conquered. It simply exists, ebbing and flowing through my life.

Over time, I've gathered tools to help me navigate it. Some are from long ago, remnants of past losses that taught me how to carry sorrow. Others are newer, shaped by the grief I hold now. Each tool helps in its own way, yet there are still moments when I find myself caught off guard—when grief appears in unexpected places, perplexing me all over again.

One of the most profound tools I've discovered on my journey of connecting with the other side is the ability to ask for guidance. I've learned that I can turn to my loved ones and my spirit guides, that I don't have to carry everything alone. And who knew? Who knew this was even possible? That when I long to speak with my mother, I truly can. That none of us are ever as alone as we might feel?

I was having a particularly challenging week when I felt the need to sit in meditation—just to be still and open to whatever messages I might receive. I grabbed my pen and journal and wrote this question:

What do I do with the dreariness?

And in return, I received these beautiful, eloquent words:

When a child dies, it brings a unique perspective to the world. Everything shifts—old beliefs, familiar routines, the way you move through your days. Sadness sheds the old, making space for joy and the new. You are unique, just as all are on their path. Grief shows up in many ways; it wants to hold your hand, even when you don't want to hold it. You quietly ignore it. You gently push it aside. But its place is in your heart. And once you place it there, it can live peacefully alongside all your other emotions.

Grief is a feeling—special and unique, indescribable. It mutates and changes as you continue to grow. Move with it, not against it. You already know how to do this in the physical sense. You pause. You wait. You observe where the other will move before you step, like a dance. Do this with grief. Allow it space and time. This is the gentlest way to "handle" grief. It does not need to be controlled. It simply wants to walk with you—for it lives within you now, forever a part of you.

Give yourself grace. Allow for mistakes. Grief will forgive you. It is loving, even when it doesn't feel that way. Blanket sadness will rise, as it does. You don't need to seek a cause. You already know why.

You will not "get over it," but you will move with it. Be with it. Surround it with your love, with your heart. In meditation, visualize grief within you and surround it with love—blues and purples and pinks, bright and warm. Nurture your grief as you have nurtured all your other emotions. Tame the ones that need taming. Grow the ones that need growing. And so it will be.

Grief does not demand to be solved. It asks only to be acknowledged, to be seen, to be felt. And in doing so, we learn that it does not have to stand in the way of love or joy—it can walk beside them. It can walk beside us.

I am still learning. This is not something I will master or complete. My tendency has always been to want to solve things, to wrap them up neatly and move on. Yet, approaching something as vast as grief in this way is new for me. It requires patience, openness, and a willingness to sit with discomfort, allowing it to coexist with love and hope.

It will be a practice—a lifelong conversation between my grief and me. And now, I know I can ask—ask for guidance, ask for space, ask for understanding from those here with me and beyond—and trust that answers will come

Part Two

Once I started listening, the signs became clearer. Specific. Surprising. Sometimes funny, sometimes so beautiful they stopped me mid-breath. These were more than coincidences—they felt like love notes from the other side. Each one was its own little miracle, reminding me that Matty was still here, just in a different way. These stories are the treasure hunts: the sacred, everyday magic of staying connected.

The Unveiling, and Everything That Showed Up First

Within Jewish tradition, there is a ritual called an *Unveiling*—a graveside ceremony where the headstone is revealed, typically a year or so after the funeral. It's meant to bring healing, a way to honor and remember.

But how does a mother prepare for something like that? How do you stand up in front of people who loved your son so deeply, your family, his friends, and say *anything* when grief still pulses just beneath the surface?

At Matty's funeral, the director, a man I've known most of my life, pulled me aside and said he had never seen so many people at a service before. I knew the unveiling would be no different.

I was grateful they would come. And, quietly dreading it.

In the weeks leading up to the day, I couldn't find the words. So, I did what had become second nature: I went into meditation and asked Matty—and those on the other side—for help. A sign. A lyric. Something I could hold onto.

That night, I woke up with words playing in my head:

Tonight I'm gonna break away, just you wait and see. I'll never be imprisoned by a faded memory. Crazy love, crazy love.

It was comforting. I whispered *Thank you* and wrote it down.

The next evening, walking Grizzly, trying to clear my mind, another lyric floated up:

Calling all angels, calling all you angels. I won't give up if you don't give up.

Full-body goosebumps. Another gift. Another whisper from beyond.

And then, as if Matty and my guides knew I needed just one more, I woke up the next morning with Tina Turner belting on loop in my mind:

You're simply the best, better than all the rest.

That one made me cry.

The night before the unveiling, I was journaling, trying to ground myself. I headed downstairs for coffee, the house full of the usual family bustle—comforting, familiar, but unmistakably missing someone.

I stepped toward the mudroom when something happened. Our iHome speaker, the one we had *never* used and had *never* set up properly, spoke out loud:

"I'm happy if you are happy."

I froze. "Did anyone else hear that?" I asked. One of my sons nodded slowly. We just stood there, soaking it in.

Another sign. Another reminder.

Later that night, in bed and wide awake, my phone buzzed. A Facebook message.

"Hi Lisa, my name is Don . . ."

I sat up in the dark, heart pounding. Don, a former lacrosse player from the late '80s at the same high school my boys attended, had walked into an ice cream shop in Connecticut *that night*, wearing a #26 shirt.

Matty's number in college was 26. It held deep significance—not just to him, but to everyone who played for that team.

A family stopped Don in the shop, recognizing the number and asking about his connection to it. He explained that he had been the Coach's first captain, the first D1 player, and #26 had always been sacred to their team.

That's when the family told him *their* story. They were Matty's cousins, and her family was on their way to Matty's unveiling the next day.

Don could've stopped there. But he went on. Back in high school, the *original* #26, E.K., had tragically passed away in a freak accident on vacation. The team vowed to carry on his legacy, wearing his number with pride. Don wore it through high school and later at his college, and he had to *fight* for it. Once he got #26, he wouldn't play without it.

Years later, he shared the story of #26 with his now-wife, and her face turned pale. She had been there. In Cancun. At the same hotel. When E.K. died.

Coincidence? Maybe. But maybe not.

That night, over ice cream, Don shared all of this with my cousin. And then, sensing the significance, he reached out to me. I thanked him, tried to express what his message meant—but I know my words fell short of the awe it stirred in me.

I printed out the conversation.

The next day, at the unveiling, I stood before the people who loved my son most. I took a deep breath.

"For 21 years, Matty showed his big, beautiful self to everyone he loved—and everyone he met. And now, even from the other side, he continues to show up. In signs. In dreams. In numbers. In ways that remind us that he's still with us. These are gifts. And I think these gifts are meant to be shared."

Then I told them about Don. And I read his message aloud. When I finished, silence filled the space. Eyes shimmered. Hands found hands. We were all feeling it: the invisible thread tying us together—across families, teams, lifetimes.

A friend of ours came up afterward and quietly said he had been in that high school class with E.K. and that they had been best friends.

I couldn't make this up if I tried.

The presence of Matty, the legacy of E.K., the echo of #26—showing up again and again, reminding us that love continues. That our people stay close. That sometimes, just when we need it, the universe hands us a story we couldn't have written better ourselves.

And maybe, just maybe, Matty wrote this one—an orchestration of connection, comfort, and awe—for his own unveiling.

Lisa Frankel

Have You Ever Noticed the Numbers?

Some signs arrive gently. A whisper. A breeze. Others . . . well, others arrive like a cartoon toddler with a club, yelling "Bamm Bamm!" and knocking everything over.

There was a cartoon I watched all the time as a kid called *The Flintstones*. It followed two prehistoric families and their children, Pebbles and Bamm Bamm. Bamm Bamm was this little boy who carried around a club—prehistoric-style—and would sometimes unin-tentionally knock over everything in sight. Other times, when he *meant* to, he'd yell "Bamm Bamm!" and go for it.

That's the image that popped into my head one day when the signs—specifically, angel numbers—started showing up again and again and again. It was like Matty was saying, *"Why don't you believe these are from me?"* and then, *"Okay then . . . I'll have to hit you over the head with them."*

I wanted signs so badly. I missed my son so much. I'd learned about angel numbers in an intuitive development class I'd taken, and I'd read about them in books on signs and the afterlife. Angel numbers are repeating number patterns. Many believe they're a little hello from the other side to remind us that we're supported and not alone.

I always believed our soul continues on after our physical body dies. It wasn't tied to any religion—I just *knew.* I'd had some early brushes with connection, with my mom, and with my grandfather. I'd seen mediums. I'd felt the truth of it.

But after Matty crossed over, the need for confirmation became fierce. The longing for connection was all-consuming. And that's when the numbers began.

At first, they came in clusters—repeating digits like 444 or 222 that would show up everywhere: license plates, receipts, street signs, clocks. They didn't just appear; they glowed. They felt . . . highlighted. And more often than not, they'd show up right in the middle of my grief, when I was in a free fall or just barely getting through the day.

One day, a few months after we moved into our new house, I was sitting in the kitchen, alone and hollow, waiting for a furniture delivery. The loss filled every inch of space. And then, my eyes drifted to the Google device on the counter: 12:21, displayed alongside a rainbow. A flutter of energy stirred in my stomach. I didn't know what it meant, but I knew it *meant* something.

Another time, while driving, I glanced at the clock: 3:33. The temperature? 33°. And just as I noticed both, Pharrell's "Happy" came on the radio. Bamm.

These moments began piling up.

I started taking photos of my morning puzzles. Completion times like 2:22, 4:44, or even 2:06—Matty's lacrosse number was 26. Bamm.

I'll never forget crying through the grocery store—holding it together just enough to check out—and seeing the total: $333.35. Bamm.

There were mornings I'd wake at exactly 5:55 or 2:26. Or 6:18—Matty's birthday. Little nudges tucked into the ordinary.

Still, even as they kept showing up, I'd ask out loud, *Matty . . . is that you?*

One morning, feeling especially low, I had to take a breathing test for my doctor. I connected to the app and checked the screen. Start time? 6:18. End time? 8:18.

Later, when I took a leap of faith and hired a business coach—no real plan, just a deep intuitive nudge—I received a text from her the night before our first call. Timestamp? 8:18. Turns out, she was two hours behind me . . . so for her, it was sent at 6:18. Bamm.

There was a season when the number 313 followed me around like a shadow. A webinar confirmation email? 3:13. Wakeups in the middle of the night? 3:13. The total at the bookstore? $33.13. Time of checkout? 3:13. It always seemed to come when I was teetering between fear and trust.

Then came a day when I had to go in for a migraine treatment—needles in my head. I was nervous, so I asked Matty to come with me. I pictured him holding my hand as I lay there. In the waiting room, I opened a word game on my phone. Final score? 81 to 81. Number of turns? 26. Time? 11:01. By the time I got back in the car, the dashboard read 12:12.

Later, I leashed up Grizzly for a walk and giggled as more than 30 dragonflies zoomed by—one even landed on me. When we got home, I finally sat down and looked at the clock. 3:13.

Bamm Bamm.

It even shows up in the tiniest of ways. I pause a show—timestamp: 8:18. Or 22:26. I reheat my coffee and glance at the timer—2:22.

Bamm Bamm.

Angel numbers. Angel winks. Whatever you call them, they fill me with wonder. They make me laugh. They make me pause. They make me feel Matty. It's like the universe whispering:

Yes. You're in tune. Keep going.

These days, I am delightfully inundated with them. And I see every one. I acknowledge them. I remain in awe. I even wrote this in my journal last week:

At the airport, sipping coffee. I check my phone—22 minutes and 2 seconds until boarding.

Seated on the plane, I glance at my return flight—it arrives at 2:22.

I go to pause my music—2:26 left on the song.

Remaining time? 44 seconds.

Driving to my mother-in-law's house, I look to my right—license plate: 818.

Watching a movie that pauses unexpectedly—time left: 22:28.

I don't need to be hit over the head anymore to believe it's him. Now, when the numbers come, I smile. I shake my head. And I whisper, "I love you."

So, I ask you—have you ever had a number tap you on the shoulder at just the right time? Do certain numbers seem to follow you? Do they make you pause, smile, or feel just a little awestruck?

Because once you start noticing . . . you'll never look at a clock the same way again.

Bamm.

The Language of 222

Learning to listen when love speaks through numbers.

N ine months. It's been nine months since you crossed over, Matty. I know grief ebbs and flows, but lately, it's been relentless—so present and so strong that it feels like a new appendage I have to learn to live with. It's awkward, clumsy, and unpredictable. Some days, I move with it; other days, it drags behind me like dead weight.

This morning, I sat with my journal and wrote: *Hello, Grief. You are ever-present yet always changing. You are strong, yet sometimes you pause. You remind me of what is. You allow anger now. You give me permission to seek solitude and quiet when I need it, to shut down entirely when I just can't do anything else.*

Time feels warped in this new reality. Logically, I know it's been nine months. But in my heart, it feels like just last week we were celebrating your 21st birthday—laughing, joking, making plans. A lifetime ago and a breath ago, all at once.

Months before you crossed over, I visited a tarot card reader who told me you were spiritually gifted and didn't seem fully grounded in the physical realm. She suggested I start paying attention to signs and symbols from the other side. I bought a small notebook to carry with me, as she had encouraged. One of the first things I wrote inside it was: *"222 means something to me."* I don't even really remember writing it. But I remember the curiosity—the feeling that there was something about 222 I was meant to notice.

I'd always seen repeating numbers, mostly from my grandfather, since I was eleven years old. I'd glance at the clock and there they were, his quiet signature of love and protection. My mother had visited me a few times, too, her voice clear in my head, guiding me to be in the right place at the right time. But I was just beginning to understand that numbers—especially 222—were more than coincidence. They were part of a language I was learning: a language of connection, of presence, of love that transcends this world and reaches into the next.

And Matty, you began teaching me this language in the most beautiful, consistent, and undeniable ways.

In the beginning, I questioned every 222 I saw—on license plates, my phone screen, timestamps, receipts. But the more they appeared, the more I trusted them as an olive branch, a whisper of reassurance, a wink from you. And oh, there were so many.

Like Graduation Weekend—a day filled with bittersweet pride and unbearable absence. Your brother Jayson was graduating from college, and you were receiving a posthumous degree from your own. Two brothers, two colleges, same day. While my sister-in-law and her husband were walking the stage for you, we were driving to celebrate Jayson. With the logistics of everything, we had to stay in a hotel overnight.

Jayson arrived first to check us in and texted the room number:

I stared at the screen, my breath catching. I showed Jeff and Justin. We all just knew. "Well," I smiled through tears, "Matty checked in first."

It was such a simple thing—just a room number. But it wasn't *just* a room number. It was you letting us know you were with us, right there, on a day that held so much meaning.

And the 222s kept coming.

The next night, my friend called, electric with excitement. She and her husband had gone to their favorite restaurant—the one they go to weekly, always sitting in the same area. But this time, the hostess turned to the server and said, "Take them to section 2, seat 22."

"They *never* say table numbers," my friend repeated. "Ever! And we've been going for years!" I smiled. You again. Clever, clever Matty.

The next day, Jayson and I got in the car to pick out a memorial tree for our new house—something that would grow with us, something symbolic of you. As I backed out of the garage, the dashboard clock blinked: 2:22. I pointed and laughed. "Look, Jays!"

Then I typed the nursery address into the GPS: 22 miles, 21 minutes. As if that weren't enough, a car changed lanes in front of us. The license plate? JS 222. (Your dad's initials.)

Jayson just smiled. "Your brother's here," I said. "And he loves the tree."

Later that evening, I booked a flight to visit my younger brother and his family. I paused before clicking "confirm." The idea of going away, even to be with people I love, made me uneasy. Would grief swallow me whole? Would I cry the whole time?

I entered my travel dates. The flight from Albany to Chicago: 2 hours, 22 minutes. Return flight: 2 hours, 2 minutes. I sat there, staring at the screen. The weight in my chest loosened. I clicked confirm and whispered, "I love you, Matty."

And still, the 222s show up. Sometimes when I least expect them, sometimes when I desperately need them. I trust each and every one to be a moment of connection with my sweet son, who now resides on the other side. This is how you talk to me.

This is how I'm learning to listen.

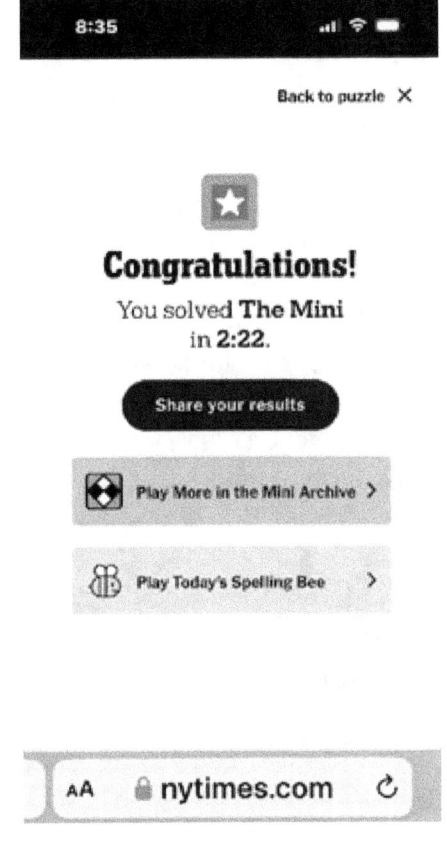

The Waiting Game: Messages in the Tiles

Some people are good at waiting. Some aren't. I've always been pretty good—able to settle in with a magazine or a book. Matty, however, was a different story.

Waiting—whether in line, at a restaurant, in a doctor's office, or for a package to arrive—felt like torture to him. So, we developed a little ritual to make the time pass: we played WordMaster, a Scrabble-like game on our phones. We only played it while waiting—it was *our* waiting game.

Matty had always shared a special bond with his great-grandma Helen. Everyone called her G. Gram. She had many great-grandchildren, but she held a soft spot for him, just as she had for me. When Matty was little, she'd watch him for an hour or so while I worked, doting on him like only a great-grandmother could. She crossed over at the age of 94.

One day, when Matty was in middle school, he and I were playing WordMaster in a doctor's office. As his letters trickled down to his board, they arranged themselves into *G Gram.*

We simply stared at each other, wide-eyed. Neither of us could speak, a rare moment for both of us!

It was just one of those little things—sweet, funny, a perfect moment of randomness.

But now, looking back, I see it differently. *They had already been showing me how to look for the magic.*

After Matty crossed over, I started receiving signs from him, many in numbers. I loved them. Seeing repeating patterns, meaningful dates, and time stamps that felt too perfect to be a coincidence reassured me that he was still with me.

Then came the dreams.

Some of our family members started having vivid dreams of Matty—not just regular dreams, but ones that felt *different*. They described them as incredibly real, unlike any dreams they'd had before. In these dreams, Matty was happy, healthy, *present*. Every time a relative had one, they'd share it with the rest of us, leaving us in awe.

Then I had one.

In my dream, I saw Matty at different ages—his cutie toddler self, his teenage self, his 21-year-old self-laughing with friends. And then, at the end, I saw something else that resembled the WordMaster tiles:

I woke up the next morning to lyrics from a Loggins & Messina song running through my mind:

"Conceived in love, sun is gonna shine above."

The signs were evolving. Matty was finding new ways to reach me.

Not long after that, my son Justin and I were sitting in an eye doctor's waiting room. We had chosen a familiar place—his best friend's mom was the doctor—but even so, the simple act of waiting in public again felt *heavy.* We were so raw.

Soft music played overhead. I wasn't really listening, just sitting there, when suddenly, I felt it—that quiet hum in my belly that told me *to pay attention.*

I turned to Justin. "This song is speaking to me," I said, though I couldn't even tell you what the song was. It just *was.*

Justin was called to the back, and I was left alone. I took a deep breath, opened my WordMaster app out of habit, and—

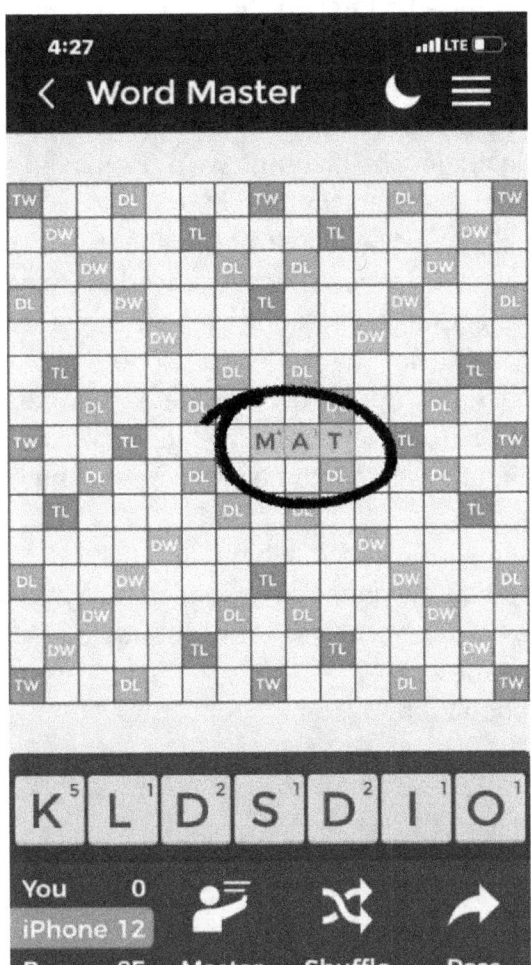

My jaw dropped. My eyes welled.

I smiled. Matty was here.

A few months later, in the dead of winter, our oldest son, Jayson, came down with a severe case of gastritis. He was in terrible pain. I called his doctor, who told us to take him to the ER.

Panic set in. The last time we'd been in an emergency room, our world had shattered.

Thankfully, a close friend called ahead to a freestanding ER a few towns over. When we arrived, we were met with warmth, kindness, and competence. They took Jayson in immediately, not because someone had called, but because that's simply how they *were*. They cared.

I held it together until they took him for advanced testing, and I was left alone in the room. That's when the wave hit me.

Nervousness. Dread. Memories. Fear.

I clutched my phone to my chest. *Matty, I know you're with us,* I whispered. *And I know it's a lot to ask, but . . . can you send me a sign?*

I opened WordMaster.

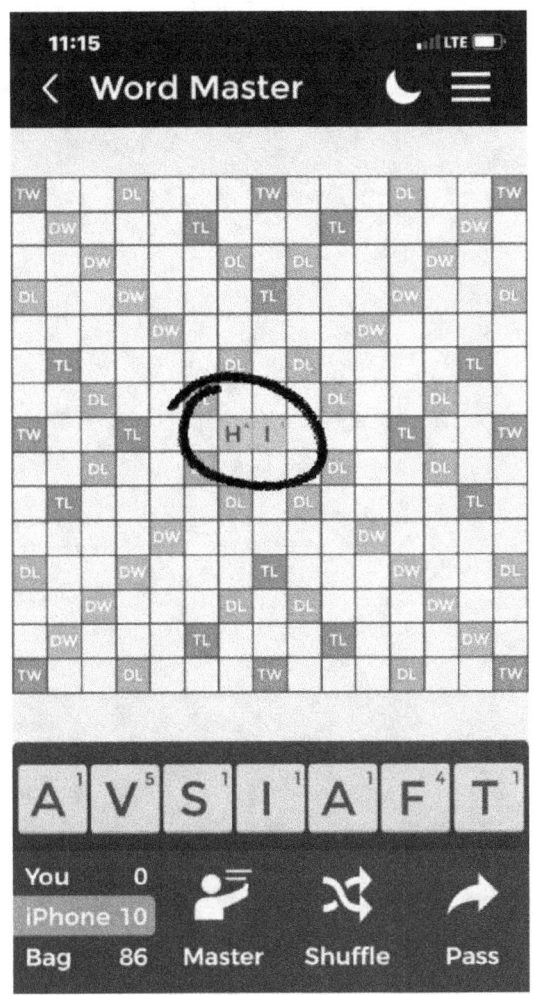

Tears. Deep breaths. There it was.

A message. A wink from Matty.

"Okay," I said aloud. *Everything's gonna be okay.* And it was.

Your First Birthday on the Other Side

Messages from Both Sides That Remind Me I'm Not Alone

June 18th, 2023—Matty's 22nd birthday. I woke up early, lying in bed, staring at the ceiling, wondering how on earth I was supposed to get through this day. But as I sat with the quiet, I made a choice—this was not going to be a day of sorrow. This was the day my beautiful, bold, fiercely kind son was born. I had hosted 21 birthdays for him. I decided: this day would hold some joy.

Still, I needed help. So I did what I often do when I need something bigger than me to lean on—I went into meditation, pen in hand, and asked Matty and the rest of my people—on the other side—for words to help me through. I closed my eyes, let my mind soften, and soon, words and images started to come: *cardinal, facts, love, smile, bee, move, Zen, birds, cherry blossoms, encouragement, forgive yourself, I'm good, cereal bowl, big bright butterfly, tricycle on driveway, laid down with me in bed, you'll be good, I had a good life, friends, you and Dad gave me a good life, brothers, soul complete, hearts, unicorn, sunshine, my only sunshine, moon and sun, rainbows and unicorns.* I wrote each word down as it came.

Each one held something. Something meaningful. A sort of shorthand between me and the people I miss.

"Sunshine, my only sunshine" was from my grandpa—he used to sing that to me when I was little. Bees? That's a sign from my mom. Rainbows? That's my dad.

And Matty? He was saying he had a good life. That I'd be okay. I wasn't sure I fully believed it yet, but I wanted to.

The tears came easily that day. But eventually, I picked up my phone and scrolled through Facebook. I wasn't sure what I was looking for—maybe something light, maybe something from Matty? Instead, I found something unexpected: dozens of "Happy Birthday!" messages.

To me.

Wait . . . what?

I stared at the screen, confused. Why was everyone wishing me a happy birthday? I scrolled, trying to make sense of it, and finally checked my profile.

My birthday had been changed to June 18th.

Seriously?

I laughed, actually laughed. Matty had shown me before that he could play with electronics, but this was a new level. I had to admit—it was a pretty good trick. And the happy birthday messages kept coming. Even though I'm not a big Facebook person, I found myself logging in to see them. It made me smile. It reminded me that people cared. That I had support. That I wasn't alone.

A few months earlier, I had asked Matty during meditation if he might add another sign to our collection, besides the numbers 26, 222, and cardinals. What came to mind was a vision of two gray pigeons. Not doves, not songbirds—just pigeons. The kind you'd expect in a city, not in our neighborhood. I kept my eyes open for them. Nothing. After a while, I stopped looking.

Later that same birthday, I took Grizzly for a walk—one of the few things that truly calms me. As we headed back, Grizzly dawdled near a house still under construction. There was a dumpster, some dirt, and right in the middle of what would one day be the driveway. Two pigeons. Just standing there. Not flying away. Not fussing. Just . . . there.

I stopped, took them in, and snapped a picture. Then I whispered, "Thank you, Matty."

That same afternoon, Christian—one of Matty's best friends—called to check in. He left me a voicemail, just making sure I was okay. The time stamp? 12:22. More of Matty's friends texted or called, too. Each one of them so thoughtful, so kind. It meant everything. These friends are pieces of Matty's heart still walking around, still showing up.

Even on the hardest days, he finds a way to remind me: I'm not doing this alone.

And maybe that was the point of the whole day.

The signs came from all directions—some subtle, some almost too obvious to believe. And somehow, through it all, I got the message.

I'm not alone—not here, and not over there.

That truth doesn't erase the ache. But it gives it somewhere to rest. And that might be what keeps me going.

Lisa Frankel

Puff, Pooh, and the Power of Signs

I really like to sing. I'm decent at it—at least, that's what people tell me. Though let's be honest, they could just be being kind. When my three boys were little, I had two go-to songs: "Puff the Magic Dragon" by Peter, Paul, and Mary and "House at Pooh Corner" by Loggins and Messina. These weren't just lullabies; they were woven into the fabric of our everyday life.

I sang them to calm my boys when they were upset, to help them settle into sleep, and even to pass the time when we were stuck in traffic. Once, I sang them over and over (and over) again while one of my sons got stitches in his chin. *Puff* and *Pooh* were my secret weapons, a musical balm for any occasion.

I've always had a soft spot for Peter, Paul, and Mary—the way their voices blend is like magic to me. I even saw them in concert once and cried on and off the entire time. When Justin was nine and away at sleepaway camp, he had the incredible experience of hearing Peter Yarrow sing in person. Turns out, Peter was an alumnus of the camp and had come back for a visit. Justin, never one to miss an opportunity, waited for his moment and ran up to Peter to tell him, *"My mom loves you!"* Cute, right? A proud moment for me—raising a kid with solid priorities.

And then there's *House at Pooh Corner*. I've always been a Winnie the Pooh fan. My boys came home from the hospital to a nursery filled with stuffed Pooh bears, and their crib sheets were covered in the Hundred Acre Wood gang. Something about those stories, those characters—there's a sweetness and a nostalgia that sneaks up on me sometimes and makes me unexpectedly emotional. We had our little rituals: watching *Winnie the Pooh* movies, cuddled up with popcorn, just soaking in the simple joys. It was *our* thing.

Years later, when I was taking my first mediumship class, we were given a homework assignment: go into meditation, ask one of our spirit guides for a sign, and make it specific. I figured, why not? So I asked for *Puff the Magic Dragon*. Our teacher said to expect it within a week.

For the first few days, I was on high alert, looking for *Puff* in every possible way. Nothing. Eventually, as these things do, the request faded to the back of my mind. Then, at the very end of the week, I found myself on the golf course with three of my friends. We play nine holes once a week at the local public course—mostly for laughs, not for any serious competition. We barely keep score.

That day, I hit a great drive—so great that I lost sight of where the ball landed. "Did anybody see where that went?" I asked.

One of my friends pointed and said, "Over by that tree, Lisa. The one that looks like a dragon. I see it as a dragon. Do you see it as a dragon? Over by the tree that looks like a dragon."

She repeated it a few times, probably because my jaw was on the ground and I was just standing there, wide-eyed. I hadn't shared the story of my spirit guide request with anyone, but at that moment, I knew. This was my sign. *Puff had arrived.* I couldn't wait to get home and write it down. Writing these moments down feels like honoring something sacred, and this? This was sacred. I've learned a lot about signs over the years. I can't predict them. I have to allow them. It's a dance—a conversation between me and spirit. I'm the recipient, and they are the creators, the deliverers. Just the other day, I was sitting in a car dealership, finalizing the purchase of my new car. There was a lot of waiting—*a lot.* I don't mind waiting as long as I have something to do, so I opened a Scrabble-like app on my phone, the same one Matty and I always played when we were stuck in waiting rooms or long lines.

As I played, I felt my lip start to twitch—something that has begun to happen when Matty is near. I love that sensation. It's like a little *hey, I'm here* from him. So I started chatting with him in my mind. *Oh, Matty, you would love this car. You'd be all over every little detail, checking out the features and deciding exactly how everything should be set up. And, yes, I upgraded just a little. Don't give me that look.* And then, as if on cue, the faint music playing in the showroom got louder. It took me a second to register, but when I did, my stomach flipped. The song? "House at Pooh

Corner." My whole body buzzed with recognition. My face broke into a huge smile. *Oh yeah, Matty's here. No denying it.*

I can't tell people enough about the power of signs and connections. They remind me—again and again—of the love that remains, of the unbreakable bond we still share. The awe, the gratitude, the deep honor I feel when these moments happen... it only grows. And maybe that's the real magic. The dragon, the bear, the melodies—they were never just songs. They were the soundtracks of our love, the echoes of a connection that even time and space can't erase. The world is filled with wonder if we're just willing to listen for the melody.

"Pooh," said Piglet, "I want you to look up at that sky, and know that, however far apart we might be physically... we are also, at the same time, together. Perhaps, more together than we have ever been before."

Beyond the Silence

Morning Lyric: *"You're not broken, just bent, and you will learn to love again."* -Pink

love being a mom. When my three boys were younger, we did everything together. I was able to stay home with them for a couple of years, and I loved every minute of it. At least once a week, we would go on what I called field trips. I'd pack us up and we'd travel to a different town to explore—playlands, parks, school playgrounds, and familiar restaurants. Each season brought its own kind of magic, like pumpkin picking in the fall or sledding in the winter. I cherish all those memories.

When the boys started school, I had the opportunity to work in their classrooms during their early elementary years. That was the best! And then, of course, they grew older. I worked, they went to school, played sports, and spent time with friends. I'm one of those moms who always felt better when I knew where my sons were. Matty, in particular, kept me in the loop. He called and texted often, letting me know what was happening and where he was—at least until he became a teenager. Then, I'm sure, there were places he went to and things he did that I didn't know about. But that's how it's supposed to be.

When I first started working with my mediumship mentor, he laughed and said that Spirit showed me as a helicopter mom. I must admit, I was a little insulted. Every mom thinks she's a *cool* mom. A helicopter mom? Sure, there were times when I needed to step in and be present, but doesn't every mom? And as Matty got older and moved away for college, I felt unbelievably honored that he still kept me in the loop as much as he did. That's why, when he crossed over, the silence was deafening.

It's been a year. And I've been given good advice— about you learning to live over there without me, and me learning to live over here without you. I've learned so much about spiritual life, and I'm sure I haven't even scratched the surface. But I've come to understand one thing: I want you to be able to move on with your spiritual life.

When you were here, I could move through my day with peace because I knew you were in peace. I used to say, *I can breathe easy when you and your brothers breathe easy.* It's always been like that for me as a mother—when my sons are settled and moving through their days with ease, I can, too. And I have been shown, gifted the feeling of, and told through mediums that *you* are in peace.

In one session, my grandfather came through and said, very clearly, *"He's over there. He's fine."* In one of my guided meditations, my mom came through and said, *"Lisa, feel his peace."* And I did. I can't describe it, but it was remarkable. I am working to trust these experiences—not only those two, but the two journals full of connections you've given me. Numbers, song lyrics, whispers in my ear, serendipitous treasure hunts. All of these moments tell me that your soul is not only peaceful but happy and thriving.

Lisa Frankel

My work is in trusting it. Trusting that you are in peace, love, and light. That you are with Spirit, surrounded by love and all of our loved ones. Every single one of them has come through to tell me you are okay. All of the tidal wave questions that once crashed over me now come in dribs and drabs, always answered by a sign, a lyric, a connection.

I know you are having adventures over there. I hope I'll be able to hear about them. Developing this new relationship, this new way of communicating, is uncharted territory. But I am so thankful that I don't have to live in that space of your absence. Your deafening absence. Instead, I get to live in the space of our new connection.

And then it dawned on me: If you were still here in the physical world, moving from 21 to 22, or 22 to 23, we would have to learn a new way of being in relationship anyway. You'd be growing up. And what if you moved overseas, and I couldn't see your happiness all the time like I did when you were younger? Would I trust your words and messages when you told me about your adventures and your happiness?

What if you were with Grandma, G. Gram, and your grandpas and great-grandfathers, and they all told me— many, many times—of your happiness and peace? Would I believe them? What if my mom were still here and connected with me over and over to say, *"He's right over there. He's fine."* Would I trust her? Of course, I would.

And if I got to visit you, to see for myself the way you're living, to see your beautiful Cheshire cat smile, to feel your hug every now and then—would it carry me until the next time I needed reassurance? I think it would.

So I ask myself, *then why not now?*

I will keep learning our new communication style. I will keep learning to raise my vibration to yours, and I know *you* are the one leading the charge... Who's the helicopter one now?

When I put down my pen after writing this, I opened my calculator to do something, and it already had a completed calculation at the top: **2,022.** I looked at the time. **5:26.**

To any mom reading this, I know how hard it is. I know the silence. But I also know that love doesn't stop at death, and neither does the connection.

65

Part Three

Before the ground gave way, there were quiet moments—some magical, some mundane—that seemed ordinary at the time. But now, I see them differently. The nudges, the whispers, the inexplicable knowings. After losing my son, the connections I had with other loved ones who had crossed over got stronger. I began to learn how to tap into it more and expand upon it. I began to realize how connected everything truly was.

Mom's Voice Inside My Head

Being a working mom of three boys meant certain seasons of life were nothing short of survival mode. I had my own business supporting and empowering others as a special educator, a parent guide, and a coach. They had school, sports, social lives—it was like running a full-time Uber service, minus the tips. But the absolute worst? The last two weeks of August. A chaotic blur of back-to-school shopping, fall sports starting up, and three kids determined to squeeze every last drop out of summer.

Eventually, I got smart. I declared those two weeks a no-work zone. Best decision I made.

One year, with my sons in 8th, 10th, and 12th grade, I found myself in unfamiliar territory—alone in the house. No one needed a ride, no one was asking what was for dinner, and for the first time in forever, I had full control of the remote. I curled up on the couch and sank into the sweet, unfamiliar bliss of doing absolutely nothing.

And then it happened.

Loud. Clear. Inside my head.

"GO TO KOHL'S!"

I sat up straight. "Okay," I said out loud, as if it were the most reasonable request in the world. I slipped on my shoes and grabbed my keys. No hesitation. No questioning it. Just pure, immediate compliance.

Because I knew—that was my mom.

And when your mom has been gone for fifteen years but suddenly yells in your head, you don't argue. You just go to Kohl's.

Halfway there, traffic slowed to a crawl. Cars were pulled off to the shoulder, and people were standing in the street. Something was wrong. I rolled down my window and asked a woman what was going on.

"A little boy ran out of the woods with no clothes on," she said, pointing toward a grassy area. "We're stopping traffic so he doesn't get hurt."

And then I saw him—darting across a front lawn. He looked about eight or nine. I didn't know him, but I recognized him. He was one of my kids. Not literally, but one of *my friends*—that's what I called the children I worked with. The ones who struggled. The ones who needed a little extra love.

My heart leapt.

I kicked off my shoes mid-sprint and took off. He spotted me and ran faster. That's when I saw a pickup truck rolling by. I locked eyes with the man in the passenger seat and shouted, "Pull over and run with me! He's fast, and I'm *not!*" To my amazement, the guy jumped out without a word and bolted after the boy.

Then came the van.

Tires screeched. A mother's panicked voice tore through the air.

"CAMERON! CAMERON!"

Cameron veered left into another yard. The guy from the truck stayed close. I followed as best I could, doing my best impression of a middle-aged gazelle.

By the time I caught up, a small crowd had gathered. No one was speaking. In the middle of it all, an older man sat on the grass, cradling Cameron gently in his lap.

Then something extraordinary happened.

Cameron lifted the man's arms, turned, and ran straight into mine. Just like that.

I held him close, whispering into his ear that he was safe, that his mama was coming. A woman from the crowd wrapped a scarf around his waist. We stood there like that—me kissing his cheek, Cameron letting me hold him like we'd always known each other.

And then she arrived. The mother whose voice had shaken the air just minutes earlier now sobbed as she clutched him, and then me. She held on as if she'd never let go. The police showed up, and as they took her statement, I helped Cameron into their van, buckled him in, and quietly handed his grandfather the number of a place that could help install bars on his bedroom window.

When the last bystander left and the sirens faded, I walked slowly back to my car. My body was shaking. My mind couldn't quite catch up to what had just happened.

I sat there for a while, staring at the steering wheel, letting the adrenaline settle.

When I finally got home, I stepped out onto the back patio and found Matty there.

"You're never gonna believe what just happened to me," I said.

I told him everything. He listened, didn't interrupt, just pulled me into a long, quiet hug.

And that was that.

My mom had yelled in my head for the first time. I listened. And because I did, I was exactly where I needed to be—to help a little boy find his way safely back to his mother.

Spiritual Choreography

Three Tiny Moments That Weren't So Tiny After All.

I used to chalk it up to luck. Being in the right place at the right time. The kind of person who caught a tray just before it toppled or stopped a toddler from toddling too far. These little moments happened often, and I never gave them much thought.

But now, I see them differently. They're not just happy accidents. They're steps in a kind of *spiritual choreography*—subtle, beautiful movements arranged by something greater. A quiet cue from Spirit. A nudge from the unseen.

I've come to believe that there's often more going on behind the scenes than we can possibly understand. Three moments confirmed this belief.

1. The Poolside Connection

For our 30th wedding anniversary, my husband and I returned to the place where we'd honeymooned. It had been a little over a year since losing our son, and while we weren't ready to celebrate in the traditional sense, we knew it would be healing to get away.

On our first day at the pool, we settled into a pair of perfect lounge chairs. By late afternoon, a large, lively group of women arrived and filled the space around us.

One woman caught my eye—adorable, with long hair, streaked purple beneath a sequined cap. When she asked, "Is this chair taken?" something shifted. The background dulled. She was in focus. *A cue.*

This happens to me sometimes. One thing lights up, and everything else fades.

A few days later, she was at the pool alone, her group was off parasailing. My husband and I joined her in the water. As we chatted, she said, "I told my spiritual coach I hear voices in my white noise machine. I can't make out the words—it just sounds like a party in the next room."

My husband's jaw dropped. Two days earlier, I'd said the exact same thing to him on the plane. Word for word.

He quietly backed away from the conversation, knowing full well what was about to happen.

We began to talk about mediumship, about energy, and Spirit. She was curious, open, ready. I felt that familiar swirl in my stomach—my signal that Spirit is near. I asked if she wanted me to connect, and when she said yes, Matty was immediately with me. That reading was the first I'd done for someone outside of my training or classes, and it was powerful.

Later that week, I read for another woman from the group. There was a natural ease to the timing of it all—like the steps of a dance we didn't know we were performing.

This wasn't random. This was spiritual choreography.

2. The Water-Walking Companion
The following year, we returned to the same spot. This time, I knew to invite Matty ahead of time to ask him for

signs. Of course, I knew he'd come anyway—but something about asking felt right.

He didn't disappoint. A dragonfly zipped by my head. *Hi, Matty.* Then a yellow butterfly. *Hi, Gram.*

I spent my afternoons walking slow laps in the pool. A friend had told me the water was shallower near the steps—valuable intel for someone my height—so I made that my route.

By day two, I'd made a pool-walking buddy. We talk to just about everyone close by on vacation, and this woman and I hit it off. We chatted, moved, and sometimes laughed over fruity drinks.

One evening, as I looped toward the deeper end, I saw a young woman standing frozen in the water. Her mother stood at the pool's edge, gently coaxing her forward. The girl was clearly nervous, struggling to move from the deep end to the steps.

I reached out my hand. "I'll walk with you," I said. "Want to take my hand?"

She looked at me, wide-eyed, and took it. We clutched my hand as we slowly made our way toward the shallower water, her mom watching from the side. When we reached the steps, she let out a deep breath. Relief, safety, trust.

It wasn't a dramatic moment, but it was meaningful. It felt like I'd been placed right there, at that exact time, for her.

And just then, another dragonfly zipped past me and hovered—lingering for a beat before flying off.

A perfectly timed cue. Another step in the dance.

3. The Dog and the Driving Route

The morning I finished writing this story, I climbed into my friend's car on our way to yoga. Before I could even buckle my seatbelt, she burst into a story:

"Thank goodness I was in the right place at the right time," she said, eyes wide.

She'd seen a little dog loose on the road near my development—two people had pulled over and were trying to catch it. She jumped in to help, using a dog toy she happened to have in her car. Eventually, they got the dog safely to its front lawn. The door opened, the dog ran inside, and the door closed behind him.

The three of them stood there for a second. No introductions. No thank-yous. Just a shared knowing that they'd been part of something good.

As she told me the story, I felt my heart smile.

I had *just* been writing about this—about no longer believing in coincidence. About being exactly where we're meant to be.

Her words echoed my own. Her timing felt like another quiet affirmation.

Not a coincidence. A cue. A continuation of the dance.

Looking Back

When I consider all three of these moments, they seem unrelated on the surface—a woman in a pool, a nervous swimmer, a loose dog on a busy road. But I see it differently.

Each one was part of a pattern. A quiet unfolding.

A choreography of spirit.

Not a performance—but a partnership. One where we learn to listen for the music, sense the steps, and trust that we're being guided through the rhythm of it all.

And maybe that's what this whole journey is about: learning to move with the mystery. Not to control it, but to *join in*.

Lisa Frankel

Connecting with My Dad

September 19, 2022

T he day started like any other, but a quiet ache lingered—a mix of missing him and the sting of our falling out years back. I'd been reading *Signs* by Laura Lynne Jackson, and it nudged me to try something. *Dad*, I thought, *show me your name today.* My father, Alan, had been gone for years, and I let the request drift away as I got on with things.

Later, I met my niece at the bridal shop for her dress fitting. It was a big moment—handing her pearls from my mom and grandma, a piece of them to carry forward. Outside, a storm was kicking up, rain pounding, wind howling. We stayed inside longer than planned, and I felt that odd buzz I'd noticed since Matty died—like static in my chest.

When we stepped out, the rain had stopped. A triple rainbow stretched across the sky, bright and clear. It hit me hard, like it was meant for me.

"Lisa, come on," I muttered. "It's just a rainbow." But it didn't feel that way. I took a few pictures, got in my car, and headed home, still feeling that hum.

I plugged in my phone, hit shuffle on Apple Music, and Madonna's "The Power to Say Goodbye" came on. My throat tightened. Then "And When I Die" by Blood, Sweat & Tears. I gripped the wheel as Peter Gabriel's "White Ashes" started—Dad's last name was White. Tears welled up.

Then Jim Croce's "I've Got a Name" played. His name. His sign.

I lost it, crying as I spoke out loud. "I hear you, Dad. The songs, your name—thank you." The playlist moved on, nothing special after that, but I didn't need more. He'd gotten through, in music, and that rainbow.

Driving home, I thought about him—how he used to take me shopping, always teasing that I was too frugal to buy anything. "Come on, kid, live a little," he'd say, grinning. Then I thought about our fight, and how dementia took him before we could fix it. Losing him twice—once to that fog, then for good—left a hole. In the car, I said what I'd held back. "Dad, I know it wasn't you. I love you. You were a great father. I was lucky."

That day, rainbows became our thing. Sometimes he sends a quarter rainbow—a splash of color on the floor or a wall where it doesn't belong. It's him, checking in, letting me know he's still around. I see it, smile, and say, "Thanks, Dad."

Lisa Frankel

Lost and Found

Morning lyric: *Don't worry about a thing, cause every little thing gonna be alright"* -Bob Marley

I never lose jewelry—*ever*. I'm the person who wears the same two bracelets, my wedding ring, and a pinky ring from my grandma every single day. I don't take them off. Not for showers, not for sleep, not for anything— because if I did, who knows where they'd end up?

Earrings, though? That's the exception. They pinch at night, so off they go—into the *same* drawer, every night, like clockwork. Because if I didn't have a system, I'd absolutely lose them. And I don't. *Ever.*

So when three of them vanished within days of each other, I was baffled. A small silver hoop, a gold earring handcrafted by someone special, and a newer light blue dangly one—each one meaningful. And each one—poof— gone. I double-checked drawers, floors, under the bed, in coat pockets, and even under the dog. Nothing.

A few mornings later, I was in my newly claimed home office, an upgrade I was pretty thrilled about. My husband, Jeff, and I had swapped spaces, and now I had the bigger room with sunlight and space for a meditation corner. It was peaceful and pretty, and apparently Grizzly's new favorite hangout spot. I was lying on the floor beside him, soaking in the calm, petting his soft ears, when Justin walked in to tell me about another one of his "uber vivid" dreams.

Since Matty crossed, Justin had been having these, like full-on, HD, surround-sound dreams. In this one, he was at work, and Matty was there in the background, just . . . hanging out. Watching him. Smiling that mischievous, knowing smile that always meant he was about to say something that made you laugh or think, or both. Justin said it felt like Matty was rooting for him. And he had drawn on that feeling ever since.

After he left the room, I stayed there on the floor with Grizzly, whispering little I love yous behind his ears. Then I looked up and said, "Thank you, Matty. Keep showing up for Justin."

And that's when I saw it. Right there on the freshly vacuumed rug—literally in front of Grizzly's fuzzy paws— was my small silver hoop. The one I had *definitely* searched for. The one that should not have been there, especially in this freshly organized, just-vacuumed, brand-new-to-me room. I stared at it. Blinked. Smiled. Of *course* it was there.

Later that same day, Jeff was in his new (smaller, darker—I may have won the office swap) workspace when he stepped on something. He bent down, picked it up, and walked into my room with a look of disbelief. "Is this yours?"

My gold earring. The handcrafted one I had lost before the move. The one that was *definitely not* on that floor the dozen times I crossed it while packing up books and taking down art. The one that had vanished. And here it was, in plain sight, waiting for him.

And then . . . the third earring.

We were sitting in the softly lit office of our grief therapist, the one who had helped us walk through the unthinkable after Matty crossed. Her space was a balm—blue and cream and soft everywhere you looked. A place where you could exhale.

In the middle of a conversation, Jeff suddenly pointed to the floor. "What's that?"

I looked. "What?"

"There. Something shiny."

And there it was. My light blue dangly earring, resting on the patterned rug like it had been gently placed there just for us to find.

All three earrings—each one holding meaning, each one lost, each one returned. One in the new office during a moment of connection. One in the old office Jeff had taken over. One in the safe, sacred space where we had worked to heal.

It was undeniable. This was more than coincidence. It was orchestrated by the unseen. Each earring a step, a beat, a nudge from Matty: *I'm here. I see you. I'm with you.*

And for the first time, Jeff saw it too.

My G. Gram Ring

I like when jewelry means something. The pieces I wear every day feel like tiny anchors to love, memory, and something greater. They stay on through showers, sleep, and seasons of life.

Among the pieces I wear every day, there's one necklace that carries a weight beyond gold: a pendant with my son's thumbprint. A gift from a beautiful friend. Who knew that when your child crosses over, you could still wear their touch against your heart? I press my thumb to his often. A silent ritual. A way to feel close. I wear it proudly as his mom, and I never take it off.

On each wrist, I have two delicate gold bangles. One belonged to my mom, who crossed over 27 years ago. The other she had made for me, melting down inherited pieces she knew she'd never wear, crafting them into something new—something lasting. She gave one to every girl in our family.

Then, there's my pinky ring. A simple silver band from my Gram. She was my biggest cheerleader, the kind of person everyone should have in their life—steady, unwavering, full of love no matter what. We were inseparable, especially when I was younger. Every year, we'd take little weekend trips together, just the two of us, filling our days with adventure and laughter. When she

81

moved into independent living in her late 80s, she began offering me small treasures, and I accepted each one, knowing they were pieces of her love.

One day, she held out the silver ring and took my hand before slipping it into my palm. "Your Grandpa surprised me with this in Mexico when we were first married," she said, eyes shining with the memory. "I wore it proudly."

Now, it was mine.

And for over a decade, it never left my hand. Through hot yoga, every shower, every swim—every everything. It stayed. Until the night it didn't.

The First Time It Left

A year before Matty crossed over, my older brother came to visit. We met at a restaurant, catching up before my husband joined us for dinner. Later that night, long after I was home, my phone buzzed.

A text. A picture.

"Is this yours?"

I stared at the image. My ring. Sitting on the floor of my brother's car.

I looked at my hand.

Oh my God.

Frantic, I texted back. *Yes. Yes. That's my G. Gram ring.*

He promised to bring it to me the next day.

I was stunned. How had it come off? Why now, after all these years?

At the time, I thought it was just a fluke. A strange accident. I had no idea it was the first whisper from the other side. A message I didn't yet understand. A reminder that they were there. That they would be there—when the unimaginable happened.

The Second Time

Nine months after Matty crossed over, I was sitting on the back porch with my dog, Grizzly. A beautiful ladybug landed beside my coffee cup. I watched it for a long time, then quietly asked, "Gram, is this a sign? Is the ladybug from you?"

The day went on, and I forgot about the moment.

Later, I took a shower, got dressed, and sat down in my bedroom chair, chatting on the phone with my younger brother.

Then I looked at my pinky.

The ring was gone.

Panic rose in my throat. "Oh my God," I said aloud. "My pinky ring is gone."

My brother kept talking, unaware of the significance. I tried to listen, but my mind raced as I searched the chair, the shower, the closet—anywhere it could have fallen.

Nothing.

After hanging up, I sat back down, heart pounding.

Matty had always been the Finder. Anytime anyone lost something, they called on him. And he found it. Always.

I took a breath.

"Matty," I asked in my mind, "can you help me find my G. Gram ring?"

I counted my breaths. Twenty of them.

Then I got up and searched again, running my foot along the rug, opening drawers, whispering, "Gram, are you trying to get my attention? Matty, will you help me find it?"

Something nudged me toward my dresser.

I walked straight to it, past the jewelry box, past the scattered keepsakes.

And there, sitting on the ring dish—the one that never holds anything, the one I've had since my wedding—was my G. Gram ring.

I hadn't put it there.

At least, not that I remembered.

I slipped it back onto my pinky, sat down hard, and whispered, "Thinking of you, Gram."

The ladybug hadn't been the sign.

The ring was.

And its message was clear: *I am always with you.*

The Third Time

Last winter, my niece came for a visit. We made lunch, sipped tea, and settled in to chat—her on the couch, me in my chair.

She was mid-sentence when I glanced down between my legs.

My breath caught.

There, on the chair between my feet, was my G. Gram ring.

"Are you kidding me?" I blurted.

My niece blinked. "What?"

I picked up the ring, slid it onto my pinky, and smiled.

"G. Gram's here," I said simply. "She's glad we're together."

Because she is. She always is.

And now, when I press my thumb to Matty's, when my bangles catch the light, when my pinky ring warms against my skin, I know—without a doubt—love never leaves us. It only finds new ways to be found.

The Finder

I love to read. And unlike the rest of the modern world, I refuse to convert to e-books. I need the weight of a book in my hands, the smell of the pages, the satisfaction of an actual bookmark instead of a glowing screen judging me for not finishing a chapter.

When my sons were younger, we spent a lot of time at the library—partly to share my love of books, partly because mandatory quiet time was a gift from the universe. Bookstores are my happy place, too. I love wandering the aisles, flipping books over to read about the authors, pretending I have enough self-control to buy just one. And whenever I travel (which isn't often), at least two books come with me.

Before a trip to visit my childhood friend and her mom, I planned a bookstore run. A friend had called to tell me about a new release by an author we both love, declaring it the best book she had *ever* read. That was all the convincing I needed. Instead of finishing what I was doing, I hopped in the car and headed straight to the store.

I found the book right away and stood in line, casually browsing overpriced trinkets when the woman in front of me turned around, gripping her earlobe.

"Did you see an earring fall?" she asked.

I hadn't, but that didn't stop me from immediately dropping to the floor like a detective on the case. We searched and searched, but no luck. She finally laughed and shrugged. "Guess I'll just buy another pair!"

As she stepped up to the counter, I felt *it*—that familiar swirl of energy in my stomach. Without thinking, I sent up a quick thought: *Okay, Matty the Finder, can you help me out here?*

In our family, Matty was *"The Finder."* Didn't matter what was lost—keys, wallets, shoes, my sanity—he could locate it in minutes, always with that little smirk like, *Really? You couldn't see this?*

So, standing in that bookstore, I closed my eyes and whispered in my head, *Move me.*

I opened my eyes, walked forward, knelt down, turned left, and reached under a shelf. My fingers closed around something small and cool.

I stood up, grinning. "I found it!"

The woman gasped and laughed. "You're a rock star!"

Nope. Not me. In my head, I told Matty, *That was all you.*

The trip was great, but when I got home, karma—or Matty's humor—kicked in. I realized I had lost my credit card. I am SO careful! And *of course*, it was *the* card. The one Matty had once taken as a preteen to buy some things, fully believing he could convince me I had simply misplaced it. His plan? "Find" it later and return it, as if he were doing me a favor. He got *busted* for that one.

I canceled the card and waited for the replacement. When it finally arrived, I flipped it over to sign the back. That's when I saw the three-digit security code: 555.

An angel number. A message. *Embrace change.*

I traced the numbers with my finger, smiling. Some things change—kids grow up, life moves forward—but some things don't. Matty is still *The Finder*. And even from the other side, he's still showing up, still helping me, still reminding me that I'm never really without him.

Spirit Has Quite the Sense of Humor

Yoga is something incredibly special to me. I've been practicing for two-thirds of my life, and I love it so much that I eventually trained to be a yoga teacher. There's just something about meditation in motion that speaks to my soul. I go every week—religiously. I used to joke that I crawl to yoga like a puzzle coming undone, and by the end, yoga puts me back together again. I'll follow good teachers wherever they go, even if it means a bit of a drive.

Lately, I've been going with a friend who's recently caught the yoga bug, and lucky for me, she drives.

One day, after class, something absolutely ridiculous happened.

During savasana, my teacher played this mesmerizing piece of music. I had never heard it before—some woman humming beautifully, almost hypnotically. It was the kind of sound that sends you into a meditative state where you forget about your to-do list, your grocery list, and even your physical body. I was completely blissed out, buzzing with energy, feeling deeply connected to something beyond myself.

Then we left the studio.

It was winter—cold, icy, the kind of day where you focus on your every step to avoid an impromptu skating routine. My friend and I were chatting as we walked to the car. I wasn't paying too much attention, just watching the ground, making sure I didn't slip. I spotted her white SUV, opened the door, and slid right in, still mid-conversation.

I glanced down at a big hunk of ice stuck behind the wheel—winter's little souvenir. And then, out of nowhere, I heard:

"Can I HELP you?"

Not in a friendly, "Oh dear, are you lost?" kind of way. More like a **"Why are you in my car, lunatic?"** kind of way.

I looked up and—yep. That was *not* my friend. That was *not* her car. And the woman in the passenger seat? ***Not happy.***

I tried to laugh it off, make a joke—something lighthearted like, "Well, I guess we're carpooling now!" But she wasn't having it. At all. I apologized, but she still looked like she was about to call 911, so I did the only logical thing: I got out and shut the door. She peeled out of the parking lot like I had just tried to carjack her.

I turned to my actual friend, who was **doubled over, gasping for air from laughing so hard.** She could barely stand.

And that was that. I went home. The day went on.

Until the next morning.

I received a long text from my sister-in-law in Chicago. She had just been at a birthday brunch with friends, complete with balloons and fun surprises. As she and her friend were leaving the restaurant, they were chatting away, and her friend gestured to the car and said, "Go ahead and get in!"

So she did.

Except . . . wrong car.

She **almost sat on the lap of a strange man. Who was also NOT happy.**

She slithered out of the car, ran to her actual friend's car, and the two of them **cried laughing.**

I nearly dropped my phone.

"You are NOT going to believe what happened to me yesterday," I texted back.

You just can't make this stuff up.

My son on the other side? Oh, he's clever. And apparently, he's got one *heck* of a sense of humor.

Lisa Frankel

A Conversation with My Father on The Other Side

Dec. 13, 2024

I move into meditation with the intention of connecting with my father and receiving understanding about his experience on the other side. It would have been his 87th birthday. He steps in warmly, with his head tilted and the shy kind of smile he wears. To provide evidence that it is him, he shows me past birthday presents we had always given him, socks and ties. I had forgotten that! He shows me a visual of myself and my brothers singing Happy Birthday to him, and he is facing us, looking at the cake and its lit candles, smiling SO broadly.

He reminds me of our back-to-school shopping trips when I was younger and shows me a particular sweater that I refused to get because it was too expensive. He loved to tell the story of how I stood firm in that. He says, "You never wanted to spend money. You were a pistol. Matty has that quality."

He shares with me that "the other side is blissful, and I get to be with loved ones, your mom, without any low-hanging emotions. Just peace." And I feel his evenness just then. It is lovely. He continues, "There are trees everywhere. Everywhere. I love that. I have juice and anything I want. Fresh. I can relax with others without feeling they have an expectation of me. My thinking is clear. Unencumbered by demon-like thoughts. Fears. I had so many fears there. I didn't realize how many until I crossed over. I love family. Mine was hard to deal with. Manage. Hard to make sense of (as you know). It's ok now over here. I see them and can be with them without trepidation or angst about how the encounter will go. All in all, it's what I wanted there but couldn't seem to get (receive)."

I ask, "Are you with Nanny and Poppy?" He replies, "Oh, yes. I love this. I am able to be with my dad in a whole new way." I ask, "How?" My dad replies, "He's a quiet man. His life held so much strife then. He's content to just BE. I like his energy now and go and just BE with him. It's tremendous, Lisa."

I ask, "Do you see the boys?" He says, "I see the boys, yes. I'm so proud of who they've become. You parented without fear and brought your Mom's philosophy into your own house, and I see the result of this now."

"Thank you, Dad."

I ask him to blend his energy with mine so I can feel his energy. He does, and I feel even and calm. He shows me the rainbow, which was his first sign to me that I took a picture of. He shows me the ¼ rainbow pin that I see and know he is with me. I thank him and tell him I love, love, love him. And off he goes.

Part Four

Grief and joy. Presence and absence. Earth and spirit. This is where I live now—within two worlds. Over time, I've learned how to keep walking forward while still holding hands with the unseen. These reflections are about integration: what it means to keep showing up for life, to feel it all, and to keep the door open to love that never ends.

I Sing the Body Electric

The first time I truly *felt* Spirit, I wasn't expecting it. It started as a swirl in my belly—an unmistakable sensation, like a shift in energy, a presence. It wasn't nerves. It wasn't anxiety. It was something more. Something *other*.

At first, I didn't know what to make of it. But then the signs kept coming. After Matty crossed over, the swirls became a nightly occurrence, a gentle but undeniable hug from my son on the other side.

I've always been sensitive to energy. Long before I understood what it meant, I could feel shifts in a room, sense emotions that weren't mine. When I worked with families and vulnerable children, I could detect a student's dysregulation in my own body before it fully surfaced in theirs. It was a skill I learned to trust—I could gauge the intensity of their emotions by how strong the sensation was in my belly, helping me choose the right approach to support them. I read books about being an empath, fascinated by the idea that someone else's energy could manifest physically in my own body.

But this? This was something else entirely.

The swirls of energy weren't connected to another person in the room. They weren't reflections of anyone's emotions. They came when I was alone, late at night, in the stillness after loss had upended my world. They came with an unmistakable feeling of love. And over time, I knew—this was Matty. This was my son, reaching across the veil to let me know he was still here.

Sometimes the energy swirls were so strong they reverberated into my limbs, and I would simply lie there, breathing through the intensity, surrendering to the visit. I always knew when it was over because, without fail, I'd break into a sweat, my body's way of saying the connection had passed. And then, every night, I'd whisper, *Thank you for the goodnight hug, Matty. I love you. Talk to you tomorrow.*

The first time a tarot reader told me I would know when Spirit was near because the upper left side of my head would tingle, I was stunned. I had never spoken that sensation aloud, yet she described it exactly. The confirmation felt like a shockwave through my system—proof that what I had been experiencing was real. After that, I began taking note. When the tingling appeared, I'd acknowledge it, say hello, and express gratitude for the visit.

Grief is an ever-unfolding process, and one day, in my journal, I described it as an onion—layered, complex, each new layer exposing something raw and unfamiliar. The outermost skin, rough and bruised, had been peeled away. What lay beneath was something different, something I didn't yet know how to navigate. But I had begun to trust the presence of my loved ones on the other side, to let that connection comfort me through each new stage of loss.

One night, as I lay in bed thinking about this unfolding process, I felt the energy swirl—Matty's hug. And for the first time, I asked out loud, "Can you make it stronger?"

It did strengthen, briefly, or at least I think it did. Then, as always, the sweat came, signaling the visit had ended. But just as I was settling back into sleep, a song lyric floated into my mind:

"I sing the body electric."

I knew that song! It was from *Fame*, a movie I had seen as a teenager. The next day, I didn't think much of it. But that night, I woke again to the same words, looping over and over in my mind:

"I sing the body electric."

The third night, it happened again. That's when it hit me—I needed to look up the full lyrics.

"I celebrate the me yet to come
I toast to my own reunion
When I become one with the sun . . ."

The words stopped me in my tracks. It was a message. A gift. A second song was added to the growing playlist Matty was sending me from the other side. I listened to it over and over, absorbing the meaning, feeling the connection, marveling at how love finds its way through.

And now, when the head tingles come or the swirl rises in my belly, I don't question it. I know.

He is here.

Over time, these sensations became more than just my personal connection with Matty. As I stepped into my role as a medium, I realized they were also part of how I connect with Spirit for others. Now, when I sit with someone longing for a sign, longing to feel their loved one near, I pay attention. The tingles, the energetic swirls, the shifts in presence—they have become my guide, my signal that a soul is near, ready to speak.

And Matty is always there, too.

At every reading, I sense him—sometimes just on the edge of my awareness, sometimes so clearly I can see him. He appears in charcoal form, his smile unmistakable. It's as if he's watching over the process, making sure everything flows just as it should. His presence is steady, reassuring, a quiet confirmation that I'm exactly where I'm meant to be.

I never could have imagined, in those first raw days of grief, that the very signs that brought me comfort would one day allow me to do the same for others. But now, I find myself in the sacred space between this world and the next, witnessing moments of profound reunion. Each time I see the relief in someone's eyes, the way their shoulders drop as they feel their loved one's presence—**I am humbled beyond words.**

It is an honor unlike any other to be entrusted with these moments of love, of healing, of remembrance.

And each time I feel that familiar swirl, I know—I am never alone in this work. Matty is here, guiding me, reminding me that love never ends.

When Your Son Becomes Your Guide

From a young age, I knew I wanted to be a teacher. At 14, I worked as a counselor-in-training at a summer camp, and I absolutely loved it. I was drawn to the kids whom others found challenging, perhaps because I've always enjoyed a challenge. My teaching style was never about standing at the front of a room and talking. I was hands-on, always finding ways to relate ideas to how each person learned best. I considered myself more of a guide. I was also a perpetual student. I've always said I'll be that gray-haired 85-year-old sitting at the front of a college lecture, eagerly taking notes, enthusiastically raising my hand, a self-proclaimed nerd through and through.

A year or so before Matty crossed over, I had stepped away from full-time work. I called it "little r" retired, not "big R" retired. I knew I'd find my next chapter. Already certified in yoga, I dove into training to teach yoga and meditation to children. And I did, briefly, until life as I knew it turned upside down.

A few months after Matty crossed over, I was lying in bed on my side. I opened my eyes and saw my husband sleeping beside me, facing the same way. And there, at the edge of the bed, was a figure. A fully formed, misty, charcoal-colored figure, outlined in shimmering emerald green. It sat, looking down at my husband.

The feeling in the room was beyond words. It radiated the deepest, most profound love and care—so immense, so pure, that I can still feel it now. I barely breathed, afraid to disturb the moment. A thought flickered in my mind, though I can't recall what it was, and I felt the being acknowledge me. Then, as if standing, it slowly dissipated.

I didn't want to forget, so I got up, went into another room, and wrote it all down. My mind raced with questions: Who was it? A loved one? A guide? An angel? Matty?

The months passed, and family members began to have vivid dreams of Matty. They described them as the most real, lifelike dreams they had ever had. But I wasn't having them. I wanted to see him—I *needed* to see him. I believed it would bring me comfort, knowing he was okay.

In the coming months, I started waking up with a vision. It was always the same — a charcoal outline of a head and shoulders, with one arm raised in a wave. At first, I dismissed it. But one morning, I woke up at exactly 4:44 AM. As I drifted back to sleep, I silently asked incredulously, *Can I see you?*

And when I woke again, eyes still closed, there he was—the same shimmering outline, waving.

I wasn't sure what to make of it, but I kept writing it all down.

I brought my journals with me when I met with my mediumship mentor. Our sessions were always powerful, though we never quite got to my journal. One day, we had to move to a different room in his shop, the very room where he had once done a reading for Matty, months before he passed. The session began, and he looked at the chair next to me. "I don't know why there's an extra chair here," he mused.

As we spoke, our conversation naturally shifted into a reading. And then he said, "Matty is sitting next to you."

He shared messages from Matty, and then my mom stepped forward as well. And finally, I asked, "How do *you* see him?"

My mentor answered, "I see a charcoal-colored figure, outlined in shimmery green."

Every bell in my head went off at once.

It was confirmation. I *had* been seeing him. What I had doubted, what I had questioned—was real.

Now, Matty is with me in every reading, in every Reiki session. He is my teacher now, my guide. Sometimes I sense him. Most often, I *see* him—that charcoal figure, doing his part on the other side to aid in healing, to bring messages for the loved ones sitting in front of me.

But it's more than that. He organizes the souls, making sure everything flows as it should. He's the one ensuring that messages come through in the right way, at the right time. Once, said with absolute certainty, *"Nobody gets to my mom without me."*

Lisa Frankel

It is something quite extraordinary when your child becomes your guide. A flipping of roles. A partnership I never imagined possible.

And yet, here we are. Doing this work together.

Who would have thought?

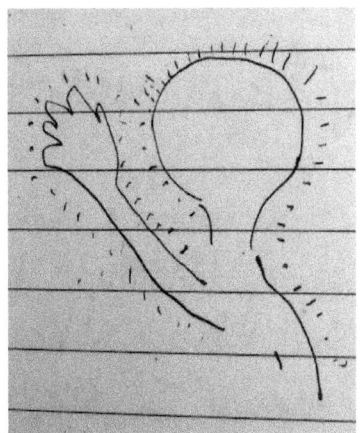

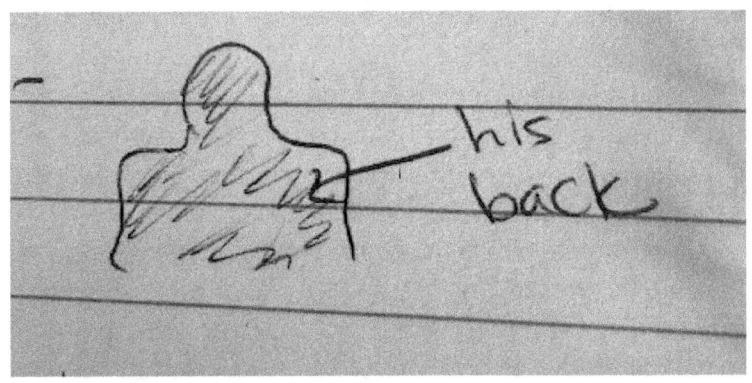

his back

Who Knew?

Grief walks beside me, always. But now and then, something happens that makes me stop in my tracks, tilt my head toward the sky, and smile through the tears. This is one of those moments.

I have lived in the Northeast all my life. It's not uncommon for it to be cold, rainy, and even snow well into April. So when the sun finally shines and the weather warms up, anybody who owns a set of golf clubs can't wait to get out on the course.

It was mid-May, and the friends I always play with and I were getting ready to head out. I was excited—the companionship of friends has helped me put aside the sadness that quietly lives inside me.

Now, I'm not exactly what you'd call a prepared athlete. I should've checked my golf bag beforehand, but our group is super casual, and it usually takes us a couple of rounds to get our groove back. So there I was, rummaging through my bag, only to find four sad, scruffy golf balls that had clearly survived last season.

One of them caught my attention: a Titleist 22.

When I picked it up, I got that feeling I've come to know. That buzzy feeling in my belly. The sense that everything else slows down for a beat, and one thing—just one— stands out. At this point, 222 was a clear sign between

Matty and me. Whenever I saw it, I knew he was with me. And in my head, I'd quietly say, *Hi honey, I love you.*

So I held up the ball and declared it my lucky ball. Off we went.

A few days before, I had felt that same buzzy presence when sitting with two friends, our feet dangling in the water of a nearby lake. One of the women and I shared a heartbreaking bond—we had both lost sons around the same age. As we sat there in quiet conversation, connecting over something no mother should ever have to go through, we kept getting soaked by splashes of cold lake water.

It was early in the season. No boats. No swimmers. The waves just . . . kept coming.

Then one of us paused. Looked around. "Wait—there are no boats, right?"

Nope. Not a one. We burst out laughing. The kind of laugh that comes from your bones. The kind that says: *You see it too, don't you?*

Two moms. Two sons on the other side. Wind, waves, and wet jeans. Who knew Spirit could control the wind?

Back on the course, we were sent out on the back 9—our favorite, though we rarely get to play it. By the time we reached the 18th hole, a par 3, I was feeling great. I hadn't lost my Titleist 22, and honestly, I'd been playing unusually well.

I teed off.

The ball soared, hit the green, and started rolling. And rolling.

My friends started yelling. I took a few steps forward to get a better look. It slowed just inches from the hole. And then, I saw him.

Matty.

Larger than life. Hovering above the green. Cartoonishly puffing out his cheeks like the Big Bad Wolf. And then—whoosh!—a gust of wind.

Just like at the lake.

The ball rolled forward, tipped, and plunked right into the hole.

We screamed. We laughed. We took so many pictures.

A guy from the pro shop came running over to document the shot. Before he left, he gave me an enthusiastic congratulations . . . and called me by the wrong name. "Congrats, Marcy!"

I didn't bother correcting him. At this point, she and I get mistaken for each other all the time—we just roll with it. The best part? She got flooded with congratulatory texts and calls all day long, despite correcting people repeatedly. We thought it was hysterical.

Matty's humor. Giving me the hole-in-one, but handing all the credit to someone else, *just to make me laugh*.

I declared it my Mother's Day gift. I just *knew* it was. And my friends knew it too—they've heard me speak about the immense connection Matty and I share.

Who knew a grieving mom could receive a Mother's Day gift from the other side?

That night, I asked Matty for a song. Something I could add to my playlist to remember this wild, beautiful gift. Something playful. Something unmistakably him.

I woke up at exactly 6:18 AM—Matty's birthdate. Then again at 6:22—his lacrosse number.

And in my head, on an endless loop, played one line: *"We may never pass this way again."*

Before I could even take it in, I heard my mom's voice pop into my head: *"He gave you a hole-in-one, and now you want a song?!"*

Yup. That's my mom.

I keep the ball in a special place with my special things. It's a reminder of the magic that can happen. Magic that sometimes wraps around my grief like a soft blanket, as I move through life holding both emotions at once.

I receive signs and connections from so many loved ones that seem to arrive just when I need them. They make me feel not alone, surrounded somehow, by love and wisdom.

Who knew?

I've come to learn that connection doesn't end when someone we love leaves this world. It changes. It stretches us. And sometimes, it surprises us in ways that feel like miracles wrapped in mischief.

This story is one of many that remind me Matty is still close, still laughing, still finding ways to reach me. I share it with the hope that it sparks a memory, a smile, or even a moment of wonder in you, too. Because if it can happen to me . . .

Who knew?

Lisa Frankel

The Branch and the Season: A Conversation with Grief

They call it a grief journey. A path. And I get that—I can visualize it. It helps me understand that there really is no end to it. I know a journey, a path, takes twists and turns, holds moments of real beauty, and sometimes, deep challenges.

I'm getting better at asking. It's never been a natural skill for me. I used to think I'd be putting others out or imposing on them. Most of the time, I'd prefer to just handle things myself. But now, I'm being guided to ask. Ask all the time. Ask so many questions of the souls on the other side, so their messages can come through, so their loved ones will know who it is.

The hardest part of asking, I'm finding, is when it's for myself. I've read so many books about grief, about the beauty of the other side, and how our angels and loved ones are simply waiting for us to ask, that it's their pleasure to answer. So, I put my hesitations aside and, once again, grab my pen and journal. I ask about a new stage of grief I feel I'm in. I ask to receive some clarity on why it makes me feel untethered and shaky.

I received these words:

You think you feel untethered due to your own circumstances at play. You are learning, which you like, and remain open to possibility and wonder: "What is next?" And yet, it doesn't matter what is next because you are only here now. Be ready here, now. Moment to moment. Ask for grief. It is ever-present, and you don't always know what to make of what you're feeling or what to call it. And that's OK. Its name is simple—Grief. The intricacies will surface, and you are advised to sit with them, to allow them to be. Like a new branch on a tree. Like a wind that blows in a new direction. Each one is unique, yet familiar in its feeling. You still call it wind. You still call it a branch. Observe it. It will be different, yet familiar. When a new season arises, you know it's a season. It's different, fresh, and new, yet you know it's spring or fall. Do not get caught up in labels or trying to figure it all out. Stay with it in the here and now, and all will be well. You have no goals with grief. You ride with it, you reside with it. It is yours to keep and hold however you so please. Those who love you, both in the physical world and beyond, hold it with you. Cherish it with you. For it is love, connection, and peace, too. Allow for the sharp edges, and make sure to see the softness it houses as well. Step aside and allow. And we will hold your hand. Love is eternal. Connection transcends the physical realm. Keep going with that. It's OK to sit in the uncertainty of this road. It is unwritten by you. Allow and trust. Be simple. Rest. Be.

As I read those words, I was struck by a new understanding, and something shifted in me. I realized that the path I walk is both familiar and new, both a change and a continuity. It's not a path to be fixed or figured out, but something to sit with and trust. As it evolves, it will be rooted in love.

And I am again shown the visual of two arms holding hands. It makes me well up. It reminds me of the connection that I never knew existed in this way.

Lisa Frankel

Two Years on the Other Side

Advice from Matty – 8/18/2024

Morning lyric: *"I hope you dance . . . I hope you dance"*

I woke up early this morning. I was excited to move into meditation to chat with you. I've just learned to converse in my Mediumship class, and this would be my first spiritual conversation with you. Grizzly and I settled in out back, in our usual spot, where it's quiet except for the birds chirping.

My questions in meditation were:
1. "Are you happy?"
2. "Did you know?"

- I have a floating sensation
- I see grandpa, gram, mom, and then dad
- They stand w/me to show me something ahead
- I see Matty, he is big and painting something
- Painting the sky white and iridescent pink
- Pink, he tells me, equals full of love
- I asked, "Did you know?"
- No, he says, not really. I suffered some. Didn't know what to make of the thoughts. Puff the Magic Dragon (in a much earlier 'meet your spirit guide'

112

meditation, I asked that my guide in some way show or tell me Puff the Magic Dragon).

He proceeds:

- with a girl
- house
- life untraveled is now
- wisdom
- family
- It's ok, Mom
- Rest assured
- It's playful
- Strange sometimes
- I'm painting a perfect blue sky
- See it . . . see love in it
- See love everywhere
- In objects, in a chair
- Remember to see love
- Forget about the bad
- It's dead and gone
- I was a limited edition
- That I knew
- Don't cry for me
- Make it bigger
- Learn
- Be free
- Tend to your human self wisely
- Continue to grow soul

I ask, "Are you painting my white bright light?"

- Yes, limitless, like the sky
- Reach out more
- Overlook . . . see out more
- Peace. Hold onto peace

I ask, "And you're fine?"

- Yes. I'm fine.
- I'm always with you. Bye.

AND NOW . . .

Morning Lyric: *"I get knocked down, but I get up again, you're never gonna keep me down . . ."*

I never imagined I would develop into a Medium. My encounters with Tarot readers and psychic mediums in my lifetime have been remarkable and profound. What I also never conceived of was working together with my youngest son after his passing. Who knew that was even a thing? Matty is always there when I connect with the Other Side in a reading and at every Reiki session.

My great Auntie Helen is my spirit guide for Tarot, always there with wisdom and support for the sitter. My mom joins almost every Reiki session. Who knew that could happen?

I no longer feel alone. My experience over these last three years has been profound in so many ways. Just this morning, I wanted advice about something happening in my life. I now go into meditation and simply ask.

I'm always so pleased with whoever shows up. The wisdom, guidance, support, and no-holds-barred messages never cease to amaze me. It's been my routine for a while to walk away from what I've written down.

Lisa Frankel

When I pick the notebook back up and read the gift that has been given in words, I am always overwhelmed with gratitude. It is always what I needed to hear.

Grief will always be a living, breathing entity that lives inside of me. It has changed me in ways I could have never anticipated. This past week was a challenging one with grief. It is Friday now, and I can feel it is settling back down to that manageable volume, one that hums quietly in the background and allows me to leave it be.

Sharing these stories has brought me peace. What I once thought was impossible—this connection, this new relationship with my son—has become part of how I live every single day. Here I am, just years after my world turned upside down, walking a path I never expected. One filled with signs, laughter, sacred pauses, and an ever-growing relationship with Spirit. License plates, things a cashier says that I know are from Matty, repeating numbers, and morning song lyrics sprinkle through my day-to-day, and I wouldn't want it any other way.

I continue to sit with people—mothers, fathers, siblings, partners, and friends who miss someone they love with everything they've got. I get to be the in-between, the go-between, the one who helps hold space as Spirit comes forward. I love it. I love watching as Spirit orchestrates the perfect thing to say or show, just when someone needs it. They're clever, tender, witty, wise, and so eager to remind us they're still right here.

My wish now is to continue doing this work. I'm not sure how my path will bend, or how I'll grow. I do know this . . . I will share the message my son is delivering:

Love is Eternal.

Connection transcends the physical realm.

Connection with our loved ones, and more, is very possible.

I never stop asking for signs. I never stop being amazed when they come.

Sometimes they crash into me like a wave—loud, laughing, and unmistakable. Other times, they slip in quietly, almost shy, as if to say, *I'm here. I'm still here.*

Each story in this collection is a gentle reminder that even when life feels ordinary, something extraordinary could be waiting just around the corner. We only have to pay attention.

Treasure hunts don't end; they simply get deeper, richer, and more full of wonder.

Thank you for walking with me through mine. I hope you find your own signs, your own moments of awe, and feel the invisible arms that still, always, hold you close.

It is profound. They are right here. This I now know.

Gratitude

To all who walked with me

I want every person reading this who knows me, even from afar, to know that you are part of this book.

I must acknowledge the immense love, support, and genuine humanity my family and I have received, and continue to receive, since the passing of our son, Matty. In the depths of our despair, we were met with a tidal wave of kindness, both grand and quiet. Hundreds and hundreds of loving, giving souls held us up, shared our sorrow, and helped us keep breathing when it felt impossible. Our community, family, and friends gave us the strength to go on. Your warmth, generosity, memories, hugs, time, and presence have been boundless. I remain awestruck—and from the depths of my heart, I thank you.

To my soul sister, Judi - thank you for walking with me through this lifetime and every lifetime before. You held space for the earliest stories and experienced the wonder of connection right alongside me, helping me trust what was possible.

To Patti, my co-navigator in it all. Your friendship has been a steady thread woven through life's chaos and joy.

To Julie, who believed in this book before I did. You listened to every sign, every connection, every song lyric, and every Treasure Hunt with unwavering presence. You cried with me, laughed with me, and helped me piece this all together. Thank you for being there for every step of this unfolding.

To my teacher, mentor, and publishers, Brandon and Daryl—thank you for helping me walk from deep sorrow into deep connection, in just the way I needed.

To my business coach, Amber, who gently guided and lovingly prodded me forward. You shared in the magic, believed in the vision, and held unwavering space for me to grow.

To my editor Catie, who shaped the words with care, and to my designer Evan, who brought the vision to light — honoring my mom's gentle whisper from beyond to 'keep it in the family' made this journey all the more meaningful.

To my family, who allowed me space on my unwritten path and supported my truth with grace and unconditional love.

To my son Matty and to all my loved ones on the Other Side, I have no words, only love.

And to you, the reader—thank you for sharing this journey. May these pages inspire you to find magic, connection, and hope in your own life.

Lisa Frankel

Meet Matty

Lisa Frankel

A car pulled in front of me at a red light

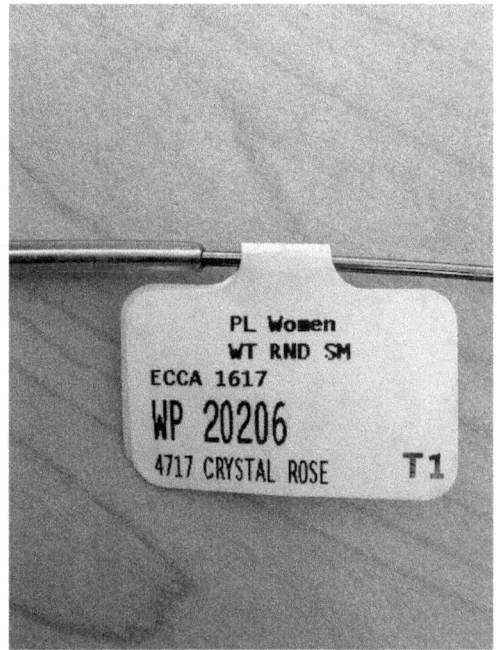

I wanted to remember which glasses frames I liked

Lisa Frankel

This Is Us
S6: E18 "Us"

I paused a TV show to answer the phone

A flashback photo of Bear on 2-2-2016

About the Author

Shiningsoulconnections.com

Lisa Frankel is an Intuitive Medium, Reiki Practitioner, parent coach, former Special Educator, and forever a seeker. Her work, whether through energy healing, spirit connection, or simple conversation—centers around holding space for others with compassion, presence, and trust in what's possible. She is the founder of Shining Soul Connections, where she supports others in finding their way forward through grief, turning points, and growth.

Treasure Hunts

Lisa lives in upstate New York with her husband Jeff and their devoted (and delightfully mischievous) dog, Grizzly. She is the mother of three sons—two who continue to light up her days from this side of life, and one whose presence lives on in her heart and across the veil, guiding her every step in quiet, wondrous ways.

www.ingramcontent.com/pod-product-compliance
Lightning Source LLC
Chambersburg PA
CBHW060046150626
46556CB00018BA/2878